By Tim Harford

The Undercover Economist
The Logic of Life
Dear Undercover Economist
Adapt
The Undercover Economist Strikes Back
Messy
Fifty Things that Made the Modern Economy

The Undercover Economist Strikes Back

How to Run – or Ruin – an Economy

TIM HARFORD

ABACUS

First published in Great Britain in 2013 by Little, Brown
This paperback edition published in 2014 by Abacus

10 9 8

A CIP catalogue record for this book
is available from the British Library

ISBN 978-0-349-13893-0

Typeset in Janson by M Rules
Printed and bound in Great Britain by
Clays Ltd, Elcograf S.p.A.

Papers used by Abacus are from well-managed forests
and other responsible sources.

MIX
Paper from
responsible sources
FSC® C104740
www.fsc.org

Abacus
An imprint of
Little, Brown Book Group
Carmelite House
50 Victoria Embankment
London EC4Y 0DZ

An Hachette UK Company
www.hachette.co.uk

www.littlebrown.co.uk

To Herbie.

Contents

The Undercover Economist Strikes Back

Introduction

1 An outlandish display

The London School of Economics, a few weeks before Christmas, 1949. The Lionel Robbins Seminar is about to begin; this prestigious event is at the razor's edge of post-war economic thought. Robbins, a giant of economics, has made the LSE a rival to John Maynard Keynes's Cambridge, recruiting future Nobel laureates such as Friedrich Hayek, John Hicks, Arthur Lewis and James Meade. But this seminar is going to be different, because Meade has persuaded Robbins to invite an unlikely speaker: a small, shy, incessantly smoking New Zealander, a mature student who has just failed in his attempt to get an honours degree in sociology.

It isn't the man – or his ever-present cigarette – which is attracting the stares. James Meade's protégé has brought with him an extraordinary device – a Heath Robinson contraption resembling an adventure playground for non-existent fish, with half a dozen or more Perspex tanks linked together through a network of pipes, dams and sluice gates and filled with water stained a deep pink with cochineal dye. It looks like what a mad genius might produce if asked to design a water clock. What any of this could possibly have to do with economics is anyone's guess. But curiosity is a powerful thing, and many of the School's finest economists are here to gawp, even to laugh, at what promises to be an outlandish display.[1]

The subject of this sudden attention, Alban William Phillips, had been born on a dairy farm in Te Rehunga in rural New Zealand thirty-five years earlier. His father, Harold, had equipped the farm with a flush toilet, a generator powered by a water-wheel, and electric light, long before the neighbouring farms had any such wonders. As a result, Bill Phillips and his siblings were able to read long into the night, at least until Harold called 'lights out', and inserted a lever into a winch in the bedroom, which pulled a wire, which pulled a chain, which – far across the farmyard night – disconnected the wheel from the generator and plunged the children's bedroom into darkness.

Harold taught his children to build crystal radios, zoetropes and toys; his wife Edith, a schoolteacher, encouraged them to study. Secondary school was nine miles away, and Bill soon became bored with cycling – so he got hold of a broken-down old truck that the adults around him regarded as being far beyond repair, and he fixed it. Aged fourteen, Bill used to drive his classmates to school, parking a discreet distance away from the eyes of his teachers.

Bill might have been expected to go to university – he passed every exam – but there was a problem. In 1929, a collapse in share prices on the stock exchange in New York, on the other side of the world, had set in motion the Great Depression. The effects lasted for years, and reached as far as a dairy farm in Te Rehunga. Prices for agricultural commodities plummeted, and Harold and Edith simply couldn't afford for their son to go to university. Bill Phillips became an apprentice electrician at a hydroelectric power station instead.

2 The birth of macroeconomics

The Great Depression caused industrial production in the United States to fall by almost half. Income per head fell by a third. The unemployment rate averaged 25 per cent through the 1930s. In an attempt to stem the bleeding in its own economy, the United States slapped punitive tariffs on imported products – with desperate consequences for countries exporting to US markets. Mass unemployment in Germany sowed the seeds of Adolf Hitler's rise. The clutching fingers of the Great Depression scrabbled all over the world.[2]

As well as changing the course of history and diverting an enterprising young New Zealander from going to university, the Great Depression profoundly revolutionised economics – how could it be otherwise? Economists asked themselves what was happening, and why, and whether anything could be done. They took new measurements, formulated new theories and proposed new policies, all concerned with the central question of economic performance as a whole. The Great Depression gave birth to macroeconomics.

A macroeconomist looks at the world through a different lens from that a microeconomist uses. Microeconomics, which I wrote about in my first two books *The Undercover Economist* and *The Logic of Life*, looks at the decisions individuals and firms make. Consider a recent visit I made to my local job centre, cheerlessly designated 'a branch of the Jobcentre Plus agency', on an appropriately miserable rainy day. A steady stream of people, young and old, male and female, were in there looking for work. The firms seeking workers had given impressive titles to the jobs, in typo-filled adverts on a chunky touch-screen terminal. The offered pay told a different story.

'Security Officer, Oxford, £7.88 to £7.88 per ho'
'Weekend Manager, Oxford, Oxfo, £7.50 per hour'
'Retail Town Supervisor, Oxford, Exceeds national mini'

How would a microeconomist view this nexus of miserable-looking jobs and miserable-looking job seekers? He would think about incentives, prices and productivity. How much is that harassed-looking young mum worth to an employer? How much is £7.50 an hour worth to her, if it means she needs to pay for childcare or loses the right to some state benefits? How much did that skinny, spotty teenager in the hoodie invest in 'human capital' at school? Are job seekers rational? Can they be 'nudged' into a more effective job search with insights from behavioural economics? (The answer, based on a randomised trial in a job centre in Loughton, near London, is 'yes'.[3])

The macroeconomist looks at this scene from quite another perspective. Instead of analysing individual firms' and job seekers' incentives, she will study the bird's eye view: the fact that there is a recession, that average wages are falling across the economy and the number of people out of work is rising. What could be the explanation for such broad changes? Some kind of shock to the system as a whole, such as an increase in the price of oil or a reduction in banks' ability to lend money, reducing the system's capacity to supply products and services? Or a loss of demand, of people's willingness to spend money on the high street? What might cause such tectonic shifts in the economic landscape? What might fix them, or prevent them? These questions seem abstract. But there can be no doubt of their importance to the lives of millions of people.

During the agonies of the Great Depression, pioneering macroeconomists fought to make sense of the intractable slump by seeking to understand the economy as a whole, and as something rather different from the sum of its parts. What this new breed of economists had in common was a sense that the economy was a thing that could break – and a thing that could be mended. The most famous among them was John Maynard Keynes, who sprang to prominence after his blistering critique of the Treaty of Versailles, *The Economic Consequences of the Peace*, and who consistently criticised the UK's economic policy throughout its depression of the 1920s. But there were others – such as Simon Kuznets, who masterminded the construction of national accounts for the United States, or Bill Phillips's mentor, James Meade, who as a student in the late 1920s abandoned his study of classics and took up economics instead, horrified by the widespread unemployment he saw around him and determined to do something. Meade later became an influential figure in the wartime governance of the British economy. All these men shared a touch of economic genius, but they also shared something else: a determination to take action.

Keynes famously declared at the beginning of the Depression that the economy was suffering from 'magneto trouble' – that is, a technical fault which might bring the entire machine grinding to a halt, but that could be fixed rather simply with the right tools and understanding. In other words, macroeconomists approached the Depression-afflicted economy in much the same way as fourteen-year-old Bill Phillips approached that forsaken old truck. Everyone else may have abandoned hope, but young Bill thought he could understand it, and fix it. And he did.

3 The Indiana Jones of economics

Back in Te Rehunga, an apprentice electrician had decided to see the world.

The *Wall Street Journal* once dubbed Steve Levitt, the co-author of *Freakonomics*, 'the Indiana Jones of economics', but if that swashbuckling label belongs to any economist, it's Bill Phillips. In between leaving New Zealand in 1935 and his first brush with economics in 1946, Phillips worked in a gold mine, hunted crocodiles, busked with a violin (he was self-taught), rode the Trans-Siberian railway, and was arrested by the Japanese and accused of spying. He eventually pitched up in London and signed up for the London School of Economics. Then the war started, and he joined the Royal Air Force, which promptly sent him back to the other side of the world.

Phillips immediately established himself as an outstanding engineer, working to upgrade the obsolete aeroplanes that were supposed to defend British-held Singapore from the Japanese. Days before Singapore surrendered, he found himself on the last convoy to flee the city, on the *Empire Star* – a refrigerated cargo ship designed to carry twenty-three passengers, but which was packed with over two thousand people, many of them women and terrified children. When the convoy was discovered and attacked by Japanese planes, Phillips found a new use for his talents as an engineer. He brought a machine gun up to the deck, and more importantly improvised a mounting for it. He then stood there for hours, fending off the attackers as bombs struck the ship around him.

This extraordinary performance earned him the MBE medal for bravery, but didn't spare him from spending more than three years in a Japanese prisoner-of-war camp. Conditions were bad. Phillips later said that the small men survived and the taller men starved; he was one of the small ones. (By the end of the war, he weighed just seven stone.) To keep everyone cheerful and up to date on news from the outside world, Phillips continued with his engineering improvisations. He built concealed radio sets, one of which was tiny enough to be hidden from the guards in the heel of his shoe. He would have been tortured and killed had it been discovered.

He also designed and built little immersion heaters, which the inmates used every evening to make hundreds of morale-boosting cups of tea. The guards never did work out why the camp lights flickered and dimmed each evening.

Although Phillips himself made light of his prison-camp experiences, it was not until many years later that the darkest episode of these years was revealed: in the summer of 1945, Phillips and thousands of other men were transferred to a death camp, where they watched the Japanese mount machine guns on the camp walls, pointing inwards, and where they were forced to dig their own mass graves. One of the other prisoners was the writer Laurens van der Post. In his memoir *The Night of the New Moon*, he describes the death camp, and a daring escapade with a 'young New Zealand officer' capable of performing 'a near miracle' with his engineering. Phillips, van der Post and another officer called Donaldson broke into the camp commander's office in search of spare parts for Phillips's tiny radio. Phillips repaired it just in time to hear the news: the Americans had dropped a bomb on Hiroshima. The end of the war was at hand.

4 The Phillips Machine

When Phillips returned to London at the end of the war, after the mother of all gap years, he simply resumed his interrupted studies at the London School of Economics. He took up sociology, a degree that contained some basic economics modules, and became intrigued by the engineering-style mathematical equations that were becoming popular in the new subject of macroeconomics. He started skipping his sociology lectures and disappearing to his landlady's garage in the London suburb of Croydon, where he put together a hydraulic representation of the equations his lecturers had been scribbling on the School's blackboards.

One of those lecturers was James Meade. Meade might easily have been taken aback when a student who had all but abandoned sociology approached him with a proposal to rework the calculus of economics as a study in plumbing. Thanks to Meade's patronage, however, Phillips was given the opportunity to demonstrate his mind-boggling machine in the exacting forum of the Robbins Seminar in late 1949. It was his big chance – his last opportunity to demonstrate that, far from being an academic failure, he had something serious to contribute to the brave new world of macroeconomics.

A cigarette never far from his lips, Phillips began his seminar by fiddling around at the back of the array of Perspex pipes and tanks and starting up a pump that had been scavenged from a Lancaster bomber. The pink-dyed water began to squirt into a tank at the top of the machine, and from there, flow down from one container to another. The pump screeched in the background like a kitchen blender as Phillips demonstrated what the machine could do.

The professors were astounded. Perhaps they would have been less so had they known more about Phillips's unorthodox education – the differential equations he'd studied by correspondence course; the hydraulic engineering he'd learned as an apprentice; the mechanical scavenging and repurposing he'd picked up on the farm and perfected in the defence of Singapore (it wasn't just the pump that was salvaged from bomber scrap; even the device's Perspex tanks were cut from the Lancaster's windows) – and of course his courage.

The machine worked perfectly. Within five minutes, the entire room was buzzing with excitement at what Phillips had created: the first ever computer model of a country's economy.

The MONIAC, or Monetary National Income Analogue Computer – these days usually just called 'The Phillips Machine' – churned out solutions to equations, using hydraulics instead of differential calculus to calculate the answers. It was a simple computer, although not quite as simple as one might assume. The machine could solve nine differential equations simultaneously and within a few minutes. Such a feat was impossible to do by hand; even in the 1950s economic models were worked out not by digital computers but by rooms full of human 'computers' – typically women armed with paper and mechanical calculators to provide the mathematical equivalent of a typing pool. It would be years before digital computers could support economic models as complex as the MONIAC's. Duplicates of the MONIAC Mark II – an expanded version of the original machine – were sold not just to Cambridge and Harvard but to ambitious governments in developing countries, and even to the Ford Motor Company.

Today, at seven feet tall and four or five feet wide, the MONIAC Mark II seems an imposing if rather quaint piece of equipment. Down the centre of the machine runs a Perspex-fronted column, intersected every foot or so with weirs and sluice gates leading off to side chambers. Column sections are neatly marked INCOME AFTER TAXES, CONSUMPTION EXPENDITURE and DOMESTIC EXPENDITURE. One compartment, the size of a small tropical fish tank, is labelled INVESTMENT FUNDS; along one wall is a curved dam made of flesh-coloured plastic, marked LIQUIDITY PREFERENCE FUNCTION. At the top corners of the machine are two spools of paper, poised to scroll gently as four pens connected to different floats wait, ready to trace lines up or down like a seismograph, recording the ebb and flow of the 'economy'. A few plastic pipes, looking for all the world as though they have been scavenged from washing machines (perhaps they were) are tucked away behind the machine. At the bottom is a large tank marked NATIONAL INCOME; a small pipe leads from that tank back to the top of the machine, from where the flow of money can begin again.

If the MONIAC was the result of exquisite engineering skill, Phillips's flash of inspiration – that hydraulics could be used to solve complex systems of equations – was close to genius. Of course, the hydraulic computer was less flexible than digital computers would eventually become. Each equation quite literally had to be carved into the flow-control system of the MONIAC, in small squares of Perspex set in a neat white frame, with a thermometer-like scale along the side. The equations themselves were slots, one in each piece of Perspex, each with a particular shape and angle, snugly holding a peg which ran smoothly on brass rails. Each peg was attached to a float and a sluice gate, so that as the water level in a tank rose, the peg would move up and – depending on the shape of the slot – would also move sideways, opening or closing the sluice gate. Phillips had carefully calibrated his equations to what was then known about the British economy: how much income people tended to put aside as savings, for example, or the overall response of supply and demand to prices in the economy. And, to his surprise, he found that the machine was watertight enough to be accurate to within 2 per cent – a higher level of precision than was required, given the likely quality of the economic statistics of the day.

To the cognoscenti, Bill Phillips's machine was more than just a brilliant technical achievement. It also embodied some ground-breaking economics. For example, when moving between an old steady state and a new one after some change in the economy, the machine produced cycles or even turbulence for a time, meticulously recorded by the rise and fall of the seismographic pens. These turbulent transitions were well ahead of the theorists, who simply had to ignore such dynamics at the time, and even now cannot fully cope with them. Another example: the MONIAC also allowed for floating exchange rates: today the dollar, the pound, the euro and the yen all have free-floating exchange rates against each other, but Bill lived in a world where countries tried to peg their currencies to each other, or to gold.

The LSE's establishment rushed to give Phillips a job. Within a decade he had been made a professor, then a very senior position in the UK; not bad for a man with no honours degree and no economics qualifications of any kind.

The MONIAC was much loved in its day, for its power as a computer and for the sheer ingenious exuberance of the thing. The machine was celebrated in the humorous magazine *Punch* – and, much later, in Terry Pratchett's novel *Making Money*. And it became an influential teaching aid: at the LSE, James Meade used to attach two MONIACs together, plugging the 'export' pipe of one into the 'import' pipe of the other, one representing the US and one the UK, to create a model of international trade. He would then invite pairs of students to play the roles of Chancellor of the Exchequer and Chairman of the Federal Reserve, manipulating interest rates or other variables in an attempt to increase the national income of their respective nations. Among the future economic policymakers who cut their teeth in Meade's lectures was perhaps the Fed's most successful chairman, Paul Volcker.

Eventually – inevitably – the MONIACs fell into disuse. An engineering professor at Cambridge, Allan McRobie, has refurbished one and it is now in full working order. The central bank of Phillips's mother country, New Zealand, also keeps a MONIAC on display. And the London School of Economics kept a machine as a teaching aid until as recently as 1992. It was then transferred to the Science Museum in London, where it sits in a great hall facing Charles Babbage's posthumously constructed Difference Engine.

5 Fixing the macroeconomic machine

The water that flows around the Phillips Machine is a good analogy for the way a macroeconomist thinks about the economy in terms of financial flows and reservoirs, of large quantities sloshing to and fro. Macroeconomists contemplate big glugs of spending power devoted to different ends: private consumption, government spending, investment, the purchase of imports. And these financial flows do not simply deepen or evaporate of their own accord, they can be dammed, redirected and siphoned off by the choices of citizens and, in particular, by the whims of the economic policymakers who can alter interest rates, taxation, or the quantity of money produced by central banks such as the Bank of England or the Federal Reserve.

Bill Phillips revolutionised the study of economics. But he didn't solve for ever the problem of how to keep the macroeconomic machine ticking over smoothly. That much is obvious from the fact that we are still suffering the consequences of the economic crisis that began in 2007. It is not as severe as the Great Depression, nor (yet) as long-lasting, but it is not absurd to make comparisons between the two events. This recession, like the Depression, has stimulated a tremendous hunger for action. We need, once again, economists with the same attitude to this dysfunctional economy that Bill Phillips had to that clapped-out truck: the attitude that we can fix it.

But to fix it, we need to understand it. And that is what this book is all about. It's not a strident call for action, nor a searing list of people to blame for the crisis. (You can find plenty of those elsewhere.) Nor is it the kind of popular economics book that offers practical ideas you can apply in your personal or business life. (You can find plenty of those elsewhere, too – including my previous books.) If it's insights into the workings of life at human scale that you're after, then quantitative easing will prove to be about as much use to you as quantum physics.

And the same applies in reverse, too: our experience of everyday life at human scale will prove of limited value when we want to understand how entire economies work. Tempting as it is to think that it would be plain common sense to run a modern economy by extrapolating from our personal experiences of running a household or a firm, we shall see that such thinking can lead us badly astray. If keeping a major economy ticking over were no more challenging than balancing a current account, I wouldn't feel the need to write this book and you wouldn't have an interest reading it.

What I have to offer in the coming pages instead is a determined and practically minded poke around under the bonnet of our economic system. I'd like us to find out, together, as much as we can about how it works. And once we've done that, I'd like us to figure out whether there is anything we can do to make it work better.

One more thing: this is a tough assignment, so I hope you won't mind that I've volunteered you to take the lead role.

1

The economy: a user's manual

'Microeconomics concerns things that economists are specifically wrong about, while macroeconomics concerns things economists are wrong about generally.'

— P.J. O'Rourke, *Eat the Rich*

Wait a minute – suddenly the economy is my problem?

Relax. It's a big responsibility, I know: an economy is for life, not just for Christmas. But you're a diligent person and you're eager to learn.

I am?

I'm sure you are, otherwise you wouldn't have bought this book. You'll do a great job.

But I've never studied economics.

Ha! You're not alone. There are a few people with their hands on the levers of the world economy who have – for instance

David Cameron, the Prime Minister, or Ben Bernanke, the chairman of the US Federal Reserve. He not only studied economics, he taught it at Princeton. But most of the world's economic movers and shakers seem happy enough without an economics degree. The Chancellor, George Osborne, has a degree in history, as did President George W. Bush. President Obama, President Hollande of France and Mariano Rajoy, Prime Minister of Spain, all studied law. Angela Merkel, the German chancellor, was a chemist.

No wonder the world economy is in such a mess. I wouldn't ask an economist to develop a new industrial chemical or defend me in court; why would a lawyer or a chemist be able to run the economy?

You're being rather kind to economists. One of the things I want to persuade you of is that while economics can help you, actually running an economy requires much more than that. John Maynard Keynes once argued that 'the master-economist must possess a rare combination of gifts ... He must be a mathematician, historian, statesman, philosopher – in some degree. He must understand symbols and speak in words. He must contemplate the particular in terms of the general, and touch abstract and concrete in the same flight of thought. He must study the present in the light of the past for the purposes of the future. No part of man's nature or his institutions must lie entirely outside his regard.'

It's not easy, but you have to admit it doesn't sound like a dull job.

Right. So – where do I start?

I've just put you in the driver's seat, so let's start by looking at the dashboard. How quickly – or slowly – is your economy ticking over? Is it speeding up or slowing down?

Fortunately, you'll have a small army of government statisticians to feed you this kind of information. That wasn't always the case. If you'll indulge me in a little historical scene-setting, governments have been trying to collect economic data for many centuries, but until quite recently the motivation was always greed: they wanted to know how rich people were so they could work out how much to tax them. Hence historical data-gathering exercises such as Caesar Augustus's famous census (the 'Census of Quirinius'), the one that apparently required Mary and Joseph to journey to Bethlehem for tax reasons two thousand years ago. The Domesday Book of 1086 was William the Conqueror's catalogue of his newly won subjects, their possessions and their taxable value. In the 1660s, William Petty produced the first estimate of a country's national income (that of the United Kingdom), as distinct from its wealth or stocks of silver and gold. Petty's number, £40 million a year, is commonly reckoned as having emerged from the very first 'national income accounts'. Intellectually, this was admirable stuff. Less admirable is that Petty had learned his trade surveying Ireland so that Oliver Cromwell could confiscate bits of it to give to his soldiers.

It was only in the 1930s, with the Great Depression – and perhaps also the possibility of war – that governments really became serious about measuring the economy with a view not to grabbing a slice of the economic pie but to fixing problems with the economic machine. (I'm not suggesting that politicians no longer want a slice of the pie; it's just that transparency and democracy have constrained such unseemly desires.) The Depression posed a new set of problems for governments, partly because it was so severe, and partly because they were more democratically accountable than they had been in the past. President Franklin D. Roosevelt, for example, was elected with the expectation that he would do something to end the economic crisis. But what? Not only was it unclear why the crisis was so deep and enduring, but it was also hard to work out the details of how the economy was performing. For example, the government might try to ease the suffering caused by unemployment by handing out welfare payments, or attack the problem directly with big infrastructure projects designed to create lots of jobs. But how much of a problem was unemployment? How many people really were unemployed? There were simply no good statistics available, and so Roosevelt's administration began to collect them.

Foremost among the economists who pioneered the modern era of collecting economic data was Simon Kuznets, who later won the Nobel prize in economics. Kuznets developed a system of 'national income accounts', a logically consistent framework for adding up all the income in the economy – or all the production, which turns out to give the same result. The centrepiece of national income accounting is a number called Gross Domestic Product, or GDP. This measures the total value of all the stuff that is produced in the economy. For example, the GDP of the world is about $70 trillion these days. All the smart phones and tablet computers, barrels of oil and kilowatt-hours of wind energy, haircuts and Brazilian waxes, sacks of rice and cartons of fried chicken wings, and everything else produced in the entire world, are collectively worth about $70 trillion a year. That's about $10,000 per person, although it's very unevenly distributed.

Hang on, though. That's just money. A Brazilian wax might have the same monetary value as the cost of a week's food for a poor family.

You're absolutely right. Actually, if the Brazilian wax is fancy enough and the family is poor enough, we might be talking about a month's worth of food. When I say 'value' and 'worth' I'm not talking about aesthetic value, or practical value, or the satisfaction these products and services might bring. Gross Domestic Product does not attempt to incorporate such slippery concepts, as reasonable people can have different subjective approaches to them. What we can measure objectively is how much money someone has shown themselves to be willing to pay for something. If a copy of the Bible sells for the same price as *Fifty Shades of Grey*, or the same price as this book, they're all the same as far as the GDP is concerned.

Isn't that a bit of a handicap? Look, if you're putting me in charge of the economy, you should know that I care more about food for the poor than Brazilian waxes.

That's very commendable. And yes, it can be a bit of a handicap; on the other hand, it's also an advantage. If, like Simon

Kuznets, you're looking for a single number to measure the size of the economy, having everything measurable on the same scale is handy. Think of it this way: it's a little bit like mass. Your brain probably weighs less than 1500 grams, and a bag of sugar typically weighs 500 grams. The fact that you value your brain more highly than three bags of sugar doesn't tell us that mass is a useless concept.

But it does tell me that if my primary concern is the welfare of my people, then I should care about something more than just GDP growth.

Quite so. I am particularly fond of one pithy quote: 'The welfare of a nation can scarcely be inferred from a measurement of national income as defined by the GDP ... goals for "more" growth should specify of what and for what.' That splendidly lucid statement came from none other than Simon Kuznets himself. The man who invented GDP never thought it was a measure of welfare, and neither should anyone else.

Of course, you might want to measure the welfare of your society more directly. And that's fine – if tricky. There are lots of competing ways to do this. You could measure 'human development', as the United Nations Development Programme does: it's a weighted average of income per head, years of education, and life expectancy. You could measure poverty rates or inequality. You could try to measure the 'subjective well-being' of your country's citizens – that is, their happiness. We'll look at all these questions in more detail in the final chapters of the book.

But for now, my point is a simple one. You're concerned about environmental damage? Great. Ever notice how rich countries generally – not always, but generally – tend to have better environments than middle-income countries? You want your people to be well educated. Good for you. Are rich countries or poor ones better placed to afford good education systems? You abhor people going hungry due to poverty. Do we tend to see more or less of that in rich countries than in poor ones? I could go on, but you get the idea. You care about things other than economic growth – but unless you're a particularly revolutionary soul, you will probably conclude that strong economic growth will give you the breathing space to think about these other things.

And while we're on the subject of rich and poor countries, let's make an important distinction between GDP and GDP per capita. If we're looking only at GDP – that is, the overall size of an economy – then we will find that the US economy is by far the world's largest. With a GDP of about $15 trillion, it's bigger than its two closest rivals put together, China (over $7 trillion) and Japan (about $6 trillion). All the European Union economies together add up to another $17 or $18 trillion, with Germany the largest; add in the remaining trillion-dollar economies – Brazil, Russia, Canada, India, Australia, Mexico and South Korea – and we've covered most of the world's economic output. But consider countries like Qatar or Switzerland. The GDP of such places is not remarkable, but their GDP per capita is enormous – significantly higher than the likes of the US, Japan and Germany, and multiples of the likes of Brazil, India and China.

Per capita, by the way, simply means per person.

Why don't economists just say 'per person'?

I think people make them nervous. But if you want more evidence that anyone who cares about people should also care about GDP, consider what happens to people in a recession. (A recession, by the way, is what we call it when GDP gets smaller for a few months; a depression is when, after such a fall, GDP keeps falling or stagnates for years.) Millions of people find themselves jobless, or trapped in jobs they hate, too fearful to leave. Unemployment hurts people far more than mere loss of income would suggest. There's a burgeoning field of 'happiness economics', and it shows that being unemployed is one of the single most depressing situations that any of us are likely to experience.

I don't think I need happiness economics to tell me that unemployment sucks.

Fair enough – although it's still important to know just how bad it is, and that it's not just a question of income. And it's important to know how bad unemployment is compared to other economic woes, such as inflation. It's really bad. The economist Arthur Okun once produced a 'misery index' by adding the unemployment rate to the inflation rate; if they were each, say, 5 per cent then the misery index would be ten. But that was just a thought experiment by Okun, and recent research shows that an extra percentage point on the unemployment rate is four times as grim as an extra percentage point on the inflation rate.[1]

You can see that these abstract-sounding numbers immediately have practical implications about how economic problems affect our quality of life. But we can also do quite down-to-earth experiments to find out more about what's really going on. For instance, in the summer of 2012, a young Lebanese Ph.D. student, Rand Ghayad of Northeastern University in Boston, used a computer program to generate 4800 resumés and mail them off to try to secure 600 advertised vacancies in different industries across the country.

I know the job market is tight but that's ridiculous.

Very funny. Actually, Ghayad only ended up studying for his Ph.D. because he graduated during a recession and, surprise surprise, couldn't get a job. But of course his mass mailout was designed to figure out what sort of candidates employers were interested in calling for interview. Those 4800 fake resumés were carefully generated to be consistent in most elements, but to vary in three ways: whether the candidate's experience was in the relevant industry or not; whether the candidate had hopped from job to job before; and whether the candidate had been unemployed for longer than six months.

Unsurprisingly, candidates with recent relevant experience were at an advantage, and a history of job-hopping did not help. But what was really striking was the effect of long-term unemployment. Applicants with experience from the wrong industry who had been unemployed for fourteen weeks or less were more than three times as likely to receive a call from the employer than applicants with experience in the right industry but who had been unemployed for six months or more. Employers are, apparently, more interested in shunning the long-term unemployed than in looking for relevant experience. And of course this is a really depressing finding, because you can see that a recession and a couple of missed opportunities can quickly drag perfectly good people away from the job market, perhaps forever. A recession does huge damage in its own right but it can also leave long-lasting scars.

Another piece of evidence comes from the economist Till Marco von Wachter, of the University of California Los Angeles. Von Wachter has studied what happens to particular groups of people trying to find jobs in tough labour markets – for instance, people who lose their jobs in a mass redundancy, or who graduate from school or college. He has found that if such people have to look for work in a recession, rather than when the economy is booming, they tend to suffer lasting damage to their earnings. Part of the problem is that people, understandably, accept jobs that aren't in the fields they really wanted to enter. They accumulate skills, experience and contacts in the wrong career. A decade after the end of the recessions he studied, von Wachter could still see differences between those who had to look for jobs in a slump and those trying to find employment in a boom.

Recessions have intangible costs, too. Benjamin Friedman, an economist at Harvard University, argues that downturns have moral consequences: as people feel insecure and unhappy, charitable donations fall, nepotism, racism and other forms of intolerance and closed-mindedness rise, and with them anti-democratic forces. The Great Depression, followed by Hitler and the Second World War, is of course the example that absorbs all the attention, but Friedman believes that the same forces are at work more subtly in gentler downturns.

This stuff matters. We should care about it. But it's not enough to care – we also need to figure out how the economy works, why it misfires, and what to do about it.

OK, so I should be trying to stop recessions. Tell me, then. Why do they happen?

If only there were a simple answer. Sometimes, it's true, there is a cause we can easily pinpoint – an economy might shrink because a country has gone through a shock like a war or a revolution or – less dramatically, but with no less impact – a sudden collapse in the price of its major exports. We'll learn more about events like that in Chapter 6. At other times, though, an economy just sickens and takes to its bed for no obvious reason. Frustratingly for economists, this happens all the time.

Let's look at Japan's recent economic history, for instance. In the early 1970s, Japan's economy grew by more than 20 per cent in just three years, after stripping out the effects of inflation. Maybe that doesn't seem like a big deal, so let's think about what it means: it's the equivalent of miraculously getting an extra day's production out of a five-day week. Quite a change over just three years. And yet in 1974, instead of putting in a fourth year of brisk growth, the Japanese economy actually shrank. Despite this blip, Japan's economy grew at about 4 per cent a year, on average, during the 1970s and 1980s. But for the past two decades, it has been growing at just

1 per cent a year. Over a couple of decades, that adds up: if it had continued to grow at 4 per cent a year, Japan would be almost twice as productive and twice as rich today. This is pretty mind-boggling.

Clearly, economists don't understand everything about how to stop an economy's growth slowing or going into reverse. If we did, it wouldn't happen, and you wouldn't be reading this book. But we have learned some things about how to understand, prevent and cure recessions. And it's how to deal with these problems that I want to spend the first two-thirds of this book talking about.

Two-thirds of a book! Crikey. Are you sure there isn't a much simpler solution that you're missing?

The world is full of people who will tell you that there is. Tie your currency to gold! Always balance your budget! Protect manufacturing! Eliminate red tape! That kind of thing. You can safely ignore these people. Anyone who insists that running a modern economy is a matter of plain common sense frankly doesn't understand much about running a modern economy.

For instance, let's consider a couple of attractively simple ideas you might hear, one from each end of the political spectrum. First, imagine that you get a left-of-centre advisor whispering in your ear that you should hire 100,000 temporary workers to undertake public works, such as digging drainage ditches. This, he argues, would boost employment and stimulate the economy. It sounds so reasonable – what could be more obvious than the idea that if you hire lots of people and put them to work, the economy will grow?

It does sound pretty reasonable, actually.

But let's not be hasty. Where will those workers come from? If you want to hire 100,000 people, there's no guarantee that you'll find 100,000 people who were just sitting around. You may find that you're competing with the private sector; people may leave their existing jobs because they like what you're offering better. Wages are likely to go up, which is nice if you have a job, but private sector companies might also replace call-centre workers with computers, street sweepers with street-sweeping machines, and supermarket staff with self-checkout machines. Or private sector firms might simply shrink, or grow more slowly than they would have done, because you're wandering around the place offering cushy jobs.

And another thing: where will the money come from to hire 100,000 people? Perhaps you plan to raise taxes; but then tax-payers will have less money in their pockets to spend. Or you could borrow, which might push interest rates up and encourage people to save money rather than spend it. Are you still so sure that this plan is reasonable?

Don't get me wrong. Your advisor's plan might work. There are certainly economic situations in which, logically speaking, it should. But there are also situations in which it would do much more harm than good. We need to know more about how the economy works before we appeal to common sense.

And in case you think that only left-wing 'common sense' is counter-productive, we could equally look at the kind of plan that would be suggested by a pro-market, right-of-centre advisor: cut taxes to stimulate the economy. Again, this seems reasonable. If you cut taxes you will leave more spending money in people's pockets, and you will also encourage people to work harder because they will keep more of the fruits of their efforts. But again, there is plenty more going on behind the scenes. If you cut taxes then for any given level of public spending you will need to borrow more money to fund public spending. Where will that borrowed money come from? It must come from somewhere, and perhaps it will come from the very same pockets of the very same people who might otherwise have paid the taxes. And perhaps they will spend less in anticipation that tax bills will eventually have to rise once you get around to plugging the hole in your government's finances.

Again, this advisor's plan might work, too. My point is that there will be twists and turns in the story as we try to figure out whether it does or not. A simple, common-sense view of the economy is attractive but dangerous, because in macroeconomics, whenever you point to some obvious change occurring right before your eyes, there is almost always something else changing behind your back, the two phenomena connected by invisible strings and pulleys.

The definitive statement of this tendency came from a French economist, essayist and parliamentarian, Frédéric Bastiat. In 1850 Bastiat published a remarkable little pamphlet with the simple title, *What Is Seen and What Is Not Seen*. Macroeconomics is all about what is not seen.

'In the economic sphere an act, a habit, an institution, a law produces not only one effect, but a series of effects. Of these effects, the first alone is immediate; it appears simultaneously with its cause; it is seen. The other effects emerge only subsequently; they are not seen; we are fortunate if we foresee them,' were Bastiat's opening words.

He then went on to describe what must be one of the most famous thought experiments in economics: whether accidentally breaking a window might stimulate the economy, as many people seem to think. It is true, of course, that broken windows increase demand for glaziers. If a child breaks a window, wrote Bastiat, then 'The glazier will come, do his job, receive six francs, congratulate himself, and bless in his heart the careless child. *That is what is seen.*'

What is not seen is the cobbler who might have received the six francs in exchange for a pair of new shoes – but does not, because the money was spent instead on replacing the window. It is easy to forget the cobbler, or shopkeeper, or landlord, or whoever else might have received the money, in part because neither we nor they will ever know they have missed out. Even the child's parents may not know: they are unlikely to have some specific alternative use in mind for the six francs. More likely, at the end of the month, they will have less in the jar of coins on the kitchen shelf, and spend less as a result.

Yet again – sorry to labour this point – it's not that breaking a window can never stimulate the economy. It could – but the chains of causation involved would be far longer and more twisted than naively contemplating the fact that the glazier has an extra six francs in his pocket.

Yes, I see. All very interesting. Look, um, it's very thoughtful of you to give me an economy to run, but – er – is there nobody else who fancies doing it?

You're not getting away that easily. Sure, macroeconomics is a subject with which we can tie ourselves in knots, if we're not careful. But the macroeconomic greats such as Phillips and Keynes were men of action: they wanted to understand the economy because they wanted to change it – to re-engineer it so that it worked better. We cannot simply collapse in a corner, sucking our thumbs and rocking backwards and forwards as we contemplate the sheer, awful complexity of the task ahead. And yet, neither must we approach 'magneto trouble' by flipping open the bonnet and whacking away at random with a hammer. We must, instead, try to understand how economies work and why, sometimes, they don't. That means understanding an economy as a system, attempting to track 'what is not seen' as well as 'what is seen'.

I can see you're feeling daunted. So let me cheer you up with an inspirational story.

2

The babysitting recession

'Since we decided a few weeks ago to adopt leaves as legal
tender, we have of course all become immensely rich ...
But, we have also run into a small inflation problem on
account of the high level of leaf availability. Which means
that I gather the current going rate has something like
three major deciduous forests buying one ship's peanut.
So, um, in order to obviate this problem and effectively
revalue the leaf, we are about to embark on an extensive
defoliation campaign, and um, burn down all the forests.'

Douglas Adams, *The Hitchhiker's Guide to the Galaxy*

The inspirational tale I have to tell concerns a recession that
began in the early 1970s, and was entirely created on Capitol
Hill, the heart of American government.

Why am I not surprised?

I'd probably better be clear about this: it wasn't an ordinary
recession in the US economy; it was a recession in a babysitting

circle called the Capitol Hill Babysitting Cooperative. The co-op was a group of parents who would babysit for each other, and most of them were members of the congressional staff who worked in or near the US Capitol – hence the co-op's name. With almost two hundred families in the circle, working out who was owed an evening of sitting, and who was owing, would have been a tricky book-keeping problem. Instead, a quasi-currency or 'scrip' was used. Families who joined the co-op were issued with forty pieces of scrip – effectively, these were like banknotes, each worth half an hour of babysitting, or fifteen minutes at specified peak times. Families exchanged these pieces of scrip with each other in return for babysitting services. If they left the co-op, they had to pay all their scrip back to the organising committee.

(If you've heard this story before, it is likely to have been from Paul Krugman, a winner of the Nobel prize in economics and now more famous as a pugnacious columnist for the *New York Times*. But there's a twist in this tale, so if you think you have heard the story already you may have a surprise in store.)

To understand the roots of the problem, imagine you're a new recruit to the co-op. You look at your forty pieces of scrip, and you think: 'Hmm. That's only ten hours of prime-time babysitting. That's not much. I was thinking of taking my partner out for a meal and a movie this weekend, but that would use up five or six hours. What if next week we got invited to some important social event at the last minute, and we didn't have enough scrip left to get emergency babysitting? On reflection, we'd better not go out this weekend. Instead, let's first put in a couple of evenings of babysitting to build up our reserves of scrip.'

Perfectly reasonable.

So reasonable that everyone else was thinking it, too. Longer-standing members of the co-op weren't any more flush with scrip themselves. In fact, because of a glitch in the way the co-op paid its administrators, the typical member had fewer than forty pieces of scrip. It wasn't just the new parents who wanted to stay in and save up some scrip – *everybody* wanted to stay in and save up some scrip. And if nobody goes out, who's going to get the chance to babysit and earn scrip? Nobody gets the chance to build up their reserves and nobody feels comfortable going out. It was a self-perpetuating circle, because each couple's income could only be the result of some other couple's spending. If there was hardly any spending then there was hardly any income either.

The result was a babysitting recession – one which can help us to think more clearly about the nature of recessions in the wider economy. Leave aside recessions caused by wars or natural disasters, and think about those curious instances where economies just take to their sick bed for no obvious reason. The underlying resources in the economy are no different. It's not like there are suddenly any fewer factories or office buildings or roads, or metals and fossil fuels under the ground. It's not as if people in the economy have suffered sudden mass amnesia about how to make things or perform services. Entrepreneurs would prefer to be employing more workers and producing more goods, and unemployed people would prefer to be earning and spending. But, for whatever reason, it just doesn't happen. Likewise, all the congressional staffers in the babysitting co-op would rather have been in a booming babysitting economy – that is, one where all were partying one weekend and babysitting the next. But it wasn't happening. Instead, everyone was mostly staying in with only their own children for company, and feeling miserable and frustrated.

The co-op was largely run by lawyers (we're talking about Washington DC here), so they tried a legalistic approach to solving the recession. 'The thinking was that some members were shirking, not going out enough, displaying the antisocial ways and morals that were destroying the co-op,' wrote Joan and Richard Sweeney in a famous short paper published in 1977 in the *Journal of Money, Credit and Banking*, the leading academic journal on the subject of monetary economics. (One of the Sweeneys was a mid-ranking Treasury official specialising in monetary research; both of them were members of the Capitol Hill Babysitting Co-op.) The co-op introduced a rule making it mandatory to go out every six months. I'm no party animal, but 'go out at least twice a year' isn't much of a lower limit. If it was intended to rev up the babysitting economy by forcing the co-op parents to liven up their social lives, things must have been desperate.

Is this my inspirational story, then? Did the rule work?

No, it didn't. But eventually, the co-op committee abandoned the ineffective legalistic tactics and switched to economics, and that did work. The solution was actually rather simple: print more money. Specifically, each member received an extra ten hours of scrip, and new members were also given an extra ten hours when they joined, but departing members only had to pay back twenty hours. The money supply, once small and shrinking, was now generous and growing. And – miracle of miracles! – the recession abated.

This is a striking story for many reasons. First, it shows that even a simple economy – a few hundred like-minded adults and a central committee with everyone's phone number and address, trading a single service – can be difficult to manage. Second, it shows that mere stories, if chosen well, can tell us quite a lot about how economies work.

But the most remarkable thing about the story is the way that monetary policy – which means altering the supply of money in the economy – cured the recession in a perfectly straightforward way. It was simple: there was a recession; a central authority conjured money from thin air (or more correctly, from thick sheets of paper); then the recession ended.

Of course the recession ended. If you can print money you can fix most economic problems, can't you? It's so easy it's cheating.

It's interesting that you think that. You're in charge of an economy yourself. You can print as much money as you like.

Really?

Sure. You don't even have to print it. You can call up your central bank, the Federal Reserve or the Bank of England or wherever, and ask the governor to add a few zeros to the sums of money held electronically in the central bank's accounts. Deciding how much money is in the economy is what central banks do.

Well – in that case, why am I reading a book about how to solve economic problems? Print the money. Problem solved.

I would have thought that the Douglas Adams quote at the beginning of the chapter would have warned you off that point of view. In his fictional economy, Fintlewoodlewix, they named the leaf as legal tender. That's a lot of money creation but it didn't do them any good. A pretty good starting point for understanding how an economy works is that production depends on the underlying resources available – labour, machinery, infrastructure. Printing money doesn't create more roads, factories or workers.

But in the babysitting co-op, printing money did solve the problem.

Yes, it did, and that's what makes the babysitting co-op such a fascinating example. Those underlying resources I was talking about were unchanged: there were parents who wanted to go out; there were parents who were willing to stay in and babysit. And yet to unlock that pre-existing potential for babysitting trades, the co-op committee had to print the correct amount of scrip – scrip which, let us remember, was nothing but a way of keeping track of who was babysitting and who was going out all the time. Printing money really did help, and rather than that fact being obvious, it should be profoundly surprising – a fact worth explaining. And explain it we shall.

But first, a word about Professor Krugman, the man who made the babysitting story famous. He once wrote that the Sweeneys' parable changed his life. 'I think about that story often; it helps me to stay calm in the face of crisis, to remain hopeful in times of depression, and to resist the pull of fatalism and pessimism.'[1]

I'm guessing that the story had such a profound effect on Krugman because – like the 'magneto trouble' metaphor of John Maynard Keynes – it taps into the idea that recessions do not have to be implacable, inevitable forces of nature. They do not have to reflect deep-seated cultural or technological problems with the structure of an economy. Recessions may well have simple, technical causes and simple, technical solutions. The Sweeneys' story exemplifies the Bill Phillips spirit: if the machine breaks down, get under the bonnet, work out what has gone wrong, and fix it.

I'm as inspired as Krugman! This is a relief – the job's looking easier than I imagined.

Ahem. Well, it's time for that twist in the tale I promised you. Unfortunately, this parable is a little bit messier than Professor Krugman's most recent retelling suggests. In his book, *End This Depression Now!*, he neglects to mention how the story ends. Alas, the ending is not a happy one. The co-op botched their monetary reform. They lurched from a situation where the stock of scrip was too small and shrinking to a situation where the stock of scrip was just perfect – but growing. As the Sweeneys put it in their original article, 'After a while, it naturally followed there was too much scrip and more people wanted to go out than to sit.'

When once nobody had been willing to go out, now nobody was willing to stay in. The end result was much the same: a babysitting recession, in which fewer evenings of babysitting were exchanged than co-op members would have wanted. Burned by their botched experiment with printing more scrip, the co-op committee refused to countenance further monetary approaches to the problem, and turned to crude legalistic tactics again. As the Sweeneys drily commented in 1977, 'a truth squad is envisaged to find out why individuals aren't sitting enough'.

Thanks a bundle. You offer me some hope, then you take it away again.

Don't be so defeatist. We can still take an optimistic view of this sorry tale. Remember that we're talking about a co-op run by Washington lawyers – there's no reason to expect them to understand monetary policy. The co-op really was a simple economy and it shouldn't have been beyond the organising committee to issue a sensible amount of scrip, if only they'd known what they were doing. We can reasonably expect that monetary authorities in the real world, staffed by experienced and educated technocrats, would do a far better job. (I think we can all agree that a bunch of lawyers on Capitol Hill are capable of mismanaging anything, and if babysitting is all that suffers we can count ourselves lucky.)

On the other hand, of course, you might point out that the Capitol Hill co-op was a rather simpler affair than a twenty-first-century economy of over 300 million citizens, totally embedded in a system of global trade, and reliant on a large and complex financial sector. Even the experienced and educated technocrats might struggle to print the right amount of scrip here. But we've decided to be optimistic, remember? Even if the details might be tricky to get right, the lesson remains: in principle you can stimulate an economy by printing money.

So we should understand why that might happen. And the fundamental reason is sticky prices.

Sticky what?

Sticky prices. Think about it. If prices adjusted with complete freedom in response to competitive forces, then the actual amount of currency in an economy simply would not matter. The babysitting co-op is a perfect case study here. Since people were desperate to babysit and accumulate scrip, and nobody wanted to go out, why didn't people offer to sit for six hours in exchange for three hours' worth of scrip? The basic problem, after all, wasn't really that people didn't have enough scrip – it was that the scrip they had didn't pay for enough babysitting. And that's a problem that could have been fixed instantly if people had felt able to ignore the face value of the scrip (thirty minutes of babysitting) and agree that the scrip was valid for an hour's sitting instead. But that didn't happen. Instead, the prices stuck.

Here's another way to think about sticky prices. Imagine you're playing a game of Monopoly and the bank runs out of money. That's not supposed to be a part of the game; the bank is allowed to run out of houses and hotels (if there was an unlimited supply the game might last for ever, rather than just feeling like it lasts for ever) but the bank is not supposed to run out of money. If you play enough games of Monopoly, though, you'll find that sometimes it happens and the game grinds to a halt. Most players respond to this awkward situation by writing paper IOUs or finding some poker chips. Hey presto! New money has been created, and the game can continue.

But there is a weird alternative: players could agree to re-denominate all the values in the game, so that £1 becomes worth £2, £5 becomes worth £10 and £500 becomes worth £1000. All rents will be halved, as will the price of property or of houses and hotels: you only need $200 to buy Boardwalk, or £200 to buy Mayfair, not 400. But because all the values change simultaneously, the real values of the properties don't change at all. This is called a 'nominal' change. Each player will simply give half her notes back to the bank, yet be none the poorer.

Logically this works just as well as creating more money. It's also the kind of thing only a Vulcan – or a classically trained economist – would suggest. Because prices do not, in fact, adjust smoothly, sometimes the central bank needs to print more money.

But why do prices stick?

Four main reasons. Here's the first. Consider the following scenario: a small photocopying shop has one employee who has worked there for six months and earns $18 an hour. Business continues to be satisfactory, but a factory in the area has closed and unemployment has increased. Other small shops have now hired reliable workers at $14 an hour to perform jobs similar to those done by the photocopy shop employee. The owner of the shop reduces the employee's wages to $14.[2]

What a jerk.

You're not the only person who thinks so. Daniel Kahneman, a psychologist who later won the Nobel prize in economics, co-wrote an article about how our sense of fairness tends to constrain what we do, and in particular how prices and wages might move. Kahneman and his colleagues presented people with the scenario above and found that 83 per cent of them thought the shop owner had been unfair, or very unfair. It's interesting that this is how our desire for fairness displays itself. After all, we could say it's unfair that this particular employee gets $18 an hour in an environment where people with similar skills only get $14 an hour. Or we could say it's unfair if the employer has to pay more than the going rate. Whatever: the point is that none of these philosophical ruminations have much emotional impact. People feel quite visceral about the idea that the employer might just cut wages from \$18 to \$14 an hour. It seems selfish and greedy.

That emotional reaction is strong enough to change the way the economy works. The shop owner, if she knows what's good for her, isn't going to cut that wage unless absolutely necessary. She feels constrained by fear of awkwardness, by her own sense of decency, or by the prospect of disruption, strike or sabotage. This kind of reluctance to cut wages is a matter of simple humanity. But it has negative consequences as well as positive ones. Perhaps the shop owner was thinking of hiring a second employee – at market wages, two staff for a total of \$28 an hour might well be better for the shop than one at \$18 an hour. But it's not going to happen; in fact, the owner might even feel unable to hire a second employee at \$14, less than the first employee gets, because arbitrary wage differences between two close colleagues are asking for trouble. It might well be better to spend the cash on a more efficient photocopying machine.

You can see why what at first looks like a question for a psychologist such as Kahneman turns out to be of great interest to you as you try to keep your economy running smoothly. Because the employer does not change the wage to reflect the market rate, supply and demand won't match up in the labour market: there will be people who want to work (say, for \$15 an hour) who can't get jobs because employers don't dare cut wages. Unemployment will be higher than it would otherwise be.

And wages aren't the only prices that might stick for reasons of perceived fairness. Kahneman and his colleagues found that their respondents were just as outraged by a scenario in which a hardware store raised the price of a snow shovel from \$30 to \$40 the night after a heavy snowstorm.

To consider a real-world example rather than a hypothetical one, think of the perennial shortage of whatever the cool new consumer gadget is. Once upon a time it was Nintendo consoles. In the mid-2000s it was Microsoft's Xbox 360. Recently it's been the latest incarnations of Apple's iPad and iPhone. Because it's hard to increase supply of a hugely popular and complex new gadget, the availability of these new products is bound to be limited. When the first batch hits the shelves, people queue around the block for them. But this is a puzzle – given high demand and limited supply, why don't companies just whack the price up? Let's say Apple can produce only 1 million iGizmos in time for Christmas; at a price of $400, they would have fully 5 million eager consumers clamouring to buy them. Wouldn't it make sense for Apple to charge a price – say, $600 – that only 1 million of those consumers would be willing to pay? Then they could reduce the price to $400 after Christmas, when more iGizmos arrive on the boat from China.

In the light of Daniel Kahneman's research, the argument against this plan is obvious: a sharp, temporary price hike would really annoy potential customers in a way that a long queue simply doesn't. And the later predictable fall in price would, similarly, annoy those who had paid the premium price at first. This isn't just a theory: in fact, Apple once tried something like this. When they launched the original iPhone, in 2007, they cut the price from $600 to $400 after two and a half months. What happened? Early adopters were infuriated, despite the fact that the higher price presumably reduced queues and shortages by dissuading other buyers. It became such a public relations nightmare for Apple, Steve Jobs quickly handed out $100 vouchers as compensation for those who had paid the higher prices.

So your point is that nobody wanted to risk social pariah status by being the first member of the co-op to say, 'I demand six hours of babysitting in return for three hours of scrip.'

Precisely. And that's only the first of our four reasons why prices can be sticky in real economies. Number two is what economists call 'menu costs'. My favourite example is the price of Coca-Cola. The price of the very first bottle of Coca-Cola, in 1886, was five cents, about a dollar in today's money. Obviously the price has gone up since then, but what is surprising is that it took more than seventy years for the price of a 6.5 oz Coke to begin that process of change. That's right: for seven decades, the price of a bottle of Coke never budged from five cents. In comparison, the price of coffee rose eight-fold over the same time.

We economists call this nominal price rigidity. My salary is not tweaked each month to reflect the latest inflation figures, and neither is yours. Restaurants do not reprint their menus (see where the term 'menu costs' comes from?) if the cost of ingredients changes by a penny, nor do wholesale companies reprint their catalogues.

It's true that Coke's nominal price rigidity was extreme; seventy years is a long time to keep the same nominal price, and over the course of that seventy-year period, Coke's costs fluctuated hugely. The company had a very good reason to stick with the five cent price: Coke was sold in vending machines that accepted only nickels. If you wanted to increase the price to six cents, you'd have had to refit every machine in the country to accept pennies as well as nickels – a task that would have been hugely expensive. So the only alternative was to put the price up to ten cents, and it would have been hard to sell a 100 per cent price hike even to the thirstiest customers. The company grew desperate: the boss of Coca-Cola wrote to his friend President Eisenhower in 1953 to suggest, in all seriousness, a 7.5 cent coin.

That's surely an extreme example.

Of course, but actually there was more to it than the vending machine story. Coke also advertised heavily that a glass of Coke cost five cents. Some of these adverts merely stuck in the mind, but others were incredibly permanent: they were on laminated drinks trays, or even vast murals on the walls of buildings. The company also distributed free Coke glasses to make sure that soda fountains didn't stint on their servings. And all this was partly because Coke had signed long-term contracts with fixed prices. And while not every company has to sell its wares through nickel-operated vending machines, many other companies also have to deal with fixed-price contracts and advertised prices that don't go away in a hurry.

It is true, however, that most companies don't wait quite so long to change prices. Researchers have tended to conclude that many prices change every year or so, and often sooner. One of the researchers who documented the Coke story, Daniel Levy, has also estimated that in the mid-1990s, it cost 52 cents to change the price of a single type of product in a supermarket. That might sound trivial, but with several hundred thousand products on the shelves such price changes added up to over $100,000 per store, and about a third of profits. In another study by Levy and his colleagues, of a large industrial equipment manufacturer, the real expense of changing prices was in management time and research, communicating the changes to the sales force, and renegotiating with customers. The total cost of changing prices was over 20 per cent of profits. Such costs won't stop prices changing for seventy years, but they may slow the process down enough to make a difference.[3]

This still sounds like mere friction rather than something substantial. Are you seriously telling me this has a real economic impact?

I could simply point out that friction is important. Try walking in a frictionless environment, for example, and let me know how it works out for you – you'll be flat on your face in half a second. Price stickiness is a lot like friction in that sense. It seems small and we might often leave it out of our models completely to keep them simple, just as a physicist would sometimes ignore friction when it would needlessly complicate an equation. But ultimately it's a big deal and the world would look very different without it.

Let me give you a simplified example to show how a small amount of price stickiness could have large effects. Imagine a world where two companies sell exactly the same product, and customers are completely aware of all price changes. Assume the product has to be priced to the nearest cent. To be specific, let's imagine we're talking about fuel and the companies are Exxon and Shell. Whichever firm has the cheapest price will get all the sales. Now imagine that Shell and Exxon can change prices only after their monthly board meetings. Shell hold theirs on the first of each month, and Exxon on the fifteenth of each month. Prices are extremely sticky, but only for a short time.

For a long time the cost of supplying fuel is 99p a litre. Exxon and Shell both sell the fuel for a pound a litre. If either of them cuts the price by another penny, they would be making zero margin and thus zero profits. If either of them *raises* the price, they would lose all customers and, again, make zero profits. By a process of elimination, the equilibrium price is a pound, with both companies making a tiny profit and (let's assume) splitting the market down the middle.

One day – let's say it's 22 February – the underlying cost of fuel falls sharply to 49p a litre.

Has somebody just struck oil in Hyde Park?

Whatever. For a few days, both companies are going to make a killing, because they can't cut their prices. They make 51p a litre – 51 times as much profit as before! – but of course on 1 March, Shell will be able to change its prices. What happens?

If Shell was colluding with Exxon, it wouldn't cut its price at all. But let's assume that there's no collusion, and that Shell simply wants to compete, to make as much money as possible with no regard whatsoever for Exxon's profits. The logical move for Shell, then, is to cut prices by a single penny, to 99p. All Exxon's customers would then buy fuel from Shell, and Shell would sell twice as much fuel for a profit of 50p a litre instead of 51p a litre, almost doubling its already stratospheric profits. Not bad. On 15 March, Exxon has its chance to respond, and we'll assume again that Exxon isn't trying to collude, but just wants to compete aggressively to make money. With the same reasoning, Exxon cuts prices to 98p a litre. It wins back all of its customers and all of Shell's, too. On 1 April, Shell cuts prices to 97p a litre. The process continues. How long before prices fall to their equilibrium level, just above cost? More than two years, despite the fact that each company has been able to adjust prices many times.

Of course this model makes some extreme assumptions, but it captures the essence of how a small amount of price stickiness can balloon into a very slow price adjustment. The key here is that each firm considers only its own profit when setting prices, not the effect on other firms. That effect can go way beyond an individual industry: if Shell cuts its price, that means more money in the pocket of every motorist, and therefore the potential for any other company in the economy to sell something to that motorist. None of that is Shell's concern, so it will cut prices more slowly than other companies would want. Each firm is strongly influenced by what other firms – suppliers and competitors – are charging.

That's reason number three for price stickiness: coordination problems. And it means that even if the obstacles to changing prices are quite small, prices may actually change surprisingly slowly.

There's a fourth and final reason for price stickiness. To illustrate it, let me tell you a true story: one day a professor received notification that his salary was being cut. Incandescent with fury, he stormed into the department head's office and threatened to quit. He was, with some effort, pacified. A few years later, the same man received another pay cut. This time, no tantrums. In fact, he was perfectly content.

Why the change of attitude?

Because the pay cut didn't look like a pay cut: it looked like a pay rise. Specifically, the professor's salary was increased by 3 per cent at a time when inflation was 6 per cent. Yet somehow a real pay cut of 3 per cent didn't seem like a pay cut at all. You can do the maths, and so could the professor – he was, after all, a professor of economics.[4] But that didn't stop him suffering from what economists call 'money illusion'. Even when we understand that we should try to take inflation into account, we may not always go to the mental effort of adjusting, and inflation-adjusted numbers often lack the emotional punch necessary to change how we behave. The raw, unadjusted numbers – we call them 'nominal wages' and 'nominal prices' – are the ones we can't help but pay attention to.

Psychological research demonstrates that nominal salaries influence our thinking even though real salaries are, logically speaking, all that should count. A nominal salary is just a number; a real salary is the goods and services that a nominal salary can buy. The money illusion explains why pay cuts in real terms are fairly common, but pay cuts in nominal terms are extremely rare – less than 0.5 per cent of salary negotiations in the United States finish with a nominal pay cut.

Remember the money illusion, by the way. It'll be useful in Chapter 4.

If you say so. But I thought this was supposed to be an inspirational chapter? All you're doing is bogging me down with reasons why my economy doesn't work smoothly.

And that's precisely why the babysitting co-op is an inspiring example.

Let's recap. All four of the reasons for price stickiness I've described could occur in a completely free-market economy. And in the real world, all successful economies have a substantial government presence that creates still further possibilities for prices to stick: regulated prices, minimum wages, public-sector pay that becomes a political football. Price stickiness is quite simply a fact of life, and it means your economy can get stuck in a rut. Imagine that, for whatever reason, your economy is shrinking. If wages and prices quickly adjust downwards, the suffering that this fall in GDP will cause is going to be contained. But if firms hesitate to cut prices because of coordination problems and menu costs, their products are going to be overpriced. Sales will fall. They will need to reduce costs, but workers will be outraged at a cut in their nominal wages, so some will be sacked instead. Unemployment will be higher than it should be, meaning that demand for goods and services will be lower, and firms will need to reduce costs more, and on, and on. Sticky prices are a recipe for trouble. Indeed, the consequences can be as severe as the Great Depression.

But the babysitting co-op points to a way out. As we saw, in the babysitting recession, willing sitters and willing party-goers were unable to exchange nights spent babysitting for one simple and silly reason – there wasn't enough scrip in circulation to enable everyone to store up the number of hours they wanted to have in reserve, and the price of babysitting was sticky. Even though the co-op botched it, the solution was there – print more money.

Got it! So you're saying that if I want to solve economic problems, I should just fire up the printing presses after all?

Yes, sometimes. It's not always a great idea, as we shall see towards the end of the next chapter. But before we get any further into the topic of creating money, I think we need to take a step back and get our heads around what money is. It turns out to be a more slippery subject than you might imagine.

3

Money, money, money

'Currency: None. Actually there are three freely
convertible currencies in the Galaxy, but none of them
count. The Altairian dollar has recently collapsed, the
Flainian Pobble Bead is only exchangeable for other
Flainian Pobble Beads, and the Triganic Pu has its own
very special problems. The exchange rate of eight Ningis
to one Pu is very easy to understand, but as a Ningi is a
triangular rubber coin six thousand eight hundred miles
on one side, nobody has ever collected enough Ningis to
own one Pu. Ningis are not convertible currency as the
Galactibanks refuse to deal in fiddling small change.
From this it may be deduced that the Galactibanks are
also the product of a deranged imagination.'

Douglas Adams, *The Restaurant at the
End of the Universe*

You wanted to talk to me about money.

I did indeed. Let me test your reaction to the following story.
On 22 August 1994, two retired musicians, Bill Drummond
and Jimmy Cauty, flew to Jura, in the Inner Hebrides off the
west coast of Scotland. They brought with them a cameraman,
a journalist (Jim Reid of the *Observer*) and twenty thousand

£50 notes, bundled and tightly wrapped in plastic bags. A million pounds. (It's worth about £1.5 million or $2.5 million in today's money.) Drummond and Cauty had, it is said, emptied their bank accounts to put the money together.

In the early hours of the next morning, the four men travelled to a remote boathouse, and with the rain hammering down outside, Cauty and Drummond made a small pile of these bundles of notes while the others acted as witnesses. Drummond and Cauty stripped out a £50 note each, lit them with a cigarette lighter, and set the rest of the money ablaze. When the dense blocks of cash would not catch, they pulled out the notes three or four at a time, crumpled them and threw them on the fire. The whole job took a couple of hours.

What a waste!

You think so? Plenty of others thought so, too. Drummond and Cauty, formerly of the hugely successful band The KLF, caused outrage. They saw their action as an artistic statement. The art world didn't seem to agree. What most people did agree on was that whether motivated by art, a desire for attention, or some rock-and-roll sense of excess, Cauty and Drummond had committed a dreadful waste of resources. The *Observer* article in which Jim Reid described what he witnessed finished with a list of what £1 million could have bought, including 'RWANDA – 2,702 kits which will feed a total of 810,810 people' and 'HOMELESS – B&B accommodation for 68 families for one year in London or 106 families outside London'.

When Drummond and Cauty appeared as guests on a television chat show, Ireland's *The Late Late Show*, hosted by Gay Byrne, they got a hostile reception as they discussed their 'art'. There were sharp questions from Byrne, and the studio audience were furious at the senseless destruction.[1] Couldn't the men have given the money to a good cause instead?

Drummond protested: 'If we'd gone and spent the money on swimming pools, Rolls Royces, I don't think people would be upset. It's because we've burned it that people are upset. And I know that this is a kind of corny thing to say and it doesn't really stand up but seeing as you're talking about the charity angle ... us burning that money doesn't mean there's any less loaves of bread in the world, any less apples, any less anything. The only thing that's less, is a pile of paper.'[2]

At that point, Byrne challenged Drummond and said that there could have been more apples or bread in the world if they'd used the money wisely. The audience applauded Byrne and jeered Drummond as he tried to continue.

You're going to tell me Byrne was wrong and Drummond was correct. Am I right?

You are indeed. The simplest way to see that is to ask how much it would have cost the Bank of England to print £1 million to replace what Drummond and Cauty incinerated. Based on what I can glean from the Bank of England (who are slightly coy but say it's 'a few pence' per banknote) and from information published by the US Federal Reserve, the cost of printing twenty thousand £50 notes would have been no more than £2000. When Drummond said that his own argument 'doesn't really stand up', he was mistaken; it stands up perfectly. And when he said that he hadn't destroyed bread or apples, only paper, he was absolutely right. All he and Cauty had destroyed was £2000 worth of paper.

In fact, far from committing a senseless waste of resources that could have gone to the needy, Drummond and Cauty had made a little gift to every one of their fellow countrymen. Instead of being outraged, people should have been thanking them.

Thanking them? For what?

Think about what happens every time the Bank of England prints extra banknotes. If there's not enough demand for goods and services to match the potential supply (and if sticky prices prevent adjustment) then the extra money should mean more demand for existing resources at the same price – this is the 'babysitting co-op' scenario we explored in the last chapter. But if people are already demanding everything that's being supplied in the economy, then prices will have to rise instead.

Flip the scenario round. If Drummond and Cauty were burning money in an economy already suffering from deficient demand – say, burning scrip in the babysitting economy – then they were making a bad situation worse. (Even then, the Bank of England could push a button at any time and reverse the damage, at a printing cost of a couple of thousand pounds.) But if, as is more likely, Drummond and Cauty were burning money in an economy where supply and demand balanced out, the resulting effect is simple to describe: average prices in the economy would drop.

They wouldn't drop much, it must be admitted. Drummond and Cauty burned £1 million at a time when there were £18,000 million of notes and coins in the hands of private individuals and companies. That number fluctuated by hundreds of millions of pounds from month to month. So the effect of Drummond and Cauty's 'art' was probably undetectable. Still, it was there in principle: something that cost £180 would, on average, have its price lowered by one penny as a result of the money burning. By shrinking the money supply by £1 million, Drummond and Cauty had effectively given £1 million away, in the form of slightly lower prices, to everybody in the world who owned some British pounds.

What a shame Drummond didn't call you for some media training.

I doubt that would have helped – it's a counter-intuitive case to make. The fundamental problem is that when we think about money, we instinctively think about individual purchasing power – about all the things that *we* could buy if *we* had that money. But from the point of view of society as a whole, things don't work like that. Drummond and Cauty destroyed £1 million worth of *their* purchasing power. But they didn't destroy £1 million worth of society's resources. Logically speaking, if you destroy your own purchasing power, but not society's purchasing power as a whole, then you must have given your purchasing power away – which is exactly what Drummond and Cauty did.

If you're going to be in charge of an economy, you need to get out of this instinctive habit of thinking about 'money' as being equivalent to 'things you could buy with the money'. For an individual, it is; for a society, it's not. As P.J. O'Rourke once said, microeconomics is about the money you don't have, while macroeconomics is about the money that the government is out of. And that's a different kind of money altogether.

Now, I hope you're not one of those readers who skip the nice quotes I've carefully chosen to put at the top of each chapter?

Er ... no. Honest.

Glad to hear it. Oddly enough, there is a near real-world equivalent to the Ningi, the triangular rubber coin larger than Mars dreamed up by the humorist Douglas Adams. It can be found on the island of Yap, in Micronesia in the West Pacific. Their coins, the *rai*, are stone wheels with a hole in the middle. Some are fairly portable – a handspan or less across, and the weight of a couple of bags of sugar. But the most valued stones are far bigger – one British sailor wrote in the late nineteenth century of a stone wheel that was four and a half tons in weight and over nine feet in diameter. In other words, it was almost completely immovable.[3]

Yap's stone money used to be a serious business. The stones were quarried and carved on the island of Palau, 250 miles away. One Victorian naturalist witnessed four hundred men from Yap, a tenth of the adult male population, at work in the quarries of Palau. Getting the stones from Palau to Yap on a little bamboo boat was a difficult and sometimes lethal affair – some of them weighed as much as two cars. (And *rai* were especially valuable if someone had died on the expedition to fetch them.) The biggest stones might have been used for major transactions such as buying land or wives; more mod- estly sized stones – a couple of feet across – were exchangeable for a pig. Even then, it would have been a lot easier to move the pig than to move the stone.

All this meant that for purely practical reasons, the Yap islanders had to develop an important monetary innovation: they divorced ownership of the stone from physical control of the object. If you wanted to buy my pig, that transaction would be publicly witnessed: I'd give you the pig and in exchange, you'd transfer ownership of one of your stones – the one leaning against the tree, second on the left behind your hut. Now everybody would know that that particular stone was Tim's stone. You and I wouldn't have to go to the trouble of actually moving the thing.

One day, a crew from the quarries were bringing a new large stone from Palau when they ran into a storm not far from the coast of Yap. The stone sank while the men swam to shore to tell the tale of their lucky escape and their loss. But of course, if the stone propped up outside your hut doesn't need to move around to change ownership, why should the stone at the bottom of the sea be any different? This giant stone on the seabed had an owner – the chief who had spon- sored the expedition to get it. And now his ownership could be transferred to another rich islander, and then to another, just as with any other stone. It was perfectly good money, even though it was out of sight and out of reach.

Yap's monetary system sounds pretty close to insane, if you ask me.

Ah, but is it? For many years the monetary systems of the developed world were based on gold. The gold itself – heavy stuff, although the ingots were not usually as heavy as a giant stone doughnut – would be left in bank vaults, after having been mined at great cost and risk from far-off lands. Naturally in an anonymous urban society such as London or Venice, nobody could use the Yap Island Honour System of 'everyone knows that's Tim's gold lying there'. But the idea was much the same. The gold, like the stone *rai*, rarely moved. It stayed in the bank vaults. People would instead carry around pieces of paper recording the fact that they owned the gold.

At first this was a purely private arrangement: a merchant with some gold would rent space in a secure vault from a goldsmith. The goldsmith would give him a note acknowledging that the gold belonged to the merchant. If the merchant wanted to buy something from a second merchant, he'd take the note to the goldsmith, collect his gold, use the gold in the trade, and then the second merchant would take the gold back to the goldsmith and collect his credit note. After a while, it became obvious that it was easier to pass around the credit notes than to go back and forth to the goldsmith all the time.

Banknotes such as the US dollar and the pound sterling

were descendants of this system. (Paper money has a much longer history, however. Kublai Khan, Chinese emperor in the thirteenth century, introduced a system of purely paper money that astounded the visiting Italian merchant Marco Polo.) Modern British and old American notes promise to pay 'the bearer on demand', a promise that once referred to redeeming the banknote in gold, just as with the private goldsmiths' banknotes. But modern currency is no longer linked to gold at all – it once was but most countries broke that link, the 'gold standard', in the early 1930s.

So why do English banknotes still say, 'I promise to pay the bearer on demand'?

It's a quaint relic of the old system. That promise no longer refers to gold – it merely means that you can go to the Bank of England and exchange a £10 note for two fivers. The Bank of England comments, 'Public trust in the pound is now maintained by the operation of monetary policy,' apparently with a totally straight face.

And that sums up the real difference between the Yap islanders and the monetary system of modern economies. On Yap, they have this crazy system where the precious stone can be perfectly good money even when it is at the bottom of the sea. In the modern world, we have a far crazier system: the precious metal can be perfectly good money even though *it isn't there at all*. We just circulate the bits of paper, with their nods and winks towards the old days when they were claims on gold in a vault. Now they are claims on nothing in particular, and somehow also claims on anything at all. Douglas Adams himself couldn't have made it up.

So if we want to think clearly about what function money serves in an economy, we should start by realising that money doesn't have to be pieces of paper or metal coins – it can be gigantic stones. Nor does it have to be intrinsically valuable. True, gold and *rai* were valued for much the same reason: they were beautiful and rare. Another early commodity money, salt, was valued for very practical reasons – it's both tasty and essential for life. Yet there are lots of intrinsically valuable items that don't make good money; a Ferrari is valuable, but not easily divisible – you can't offer one of its wheels in exchange for a holiday. Moreover, something can function perfectly well as money without having much intrinsic value at all – as we have seen, anyone who conducts business in British pounds would be quite happy to hand over £1 million worth of goods in return for printed paper worth only a couple of thousand. Money systems such as the goldsmith's notes were initially anchored to an intrinsically valuable commodity, but against all intuition that valuable commodity turned out to be unnecessary. All that is necessary for money to have value is for everyone to believe that it has value.

Right. How do you achieve that?

The textbook view of money is that it has three roles: as a medium of exchange, a store of value, and a unit of account. As we'll see, each of these functions can in some circumstances be peeled away from the others, but the best money will have all three together.

Let's take each role in turn. A medium of exchange is a way of keeping track of transactions. In modern societies, paper money is a medium of exchange. If I can supply laundry services and I want a new computer, I don't have to find a computer retailer who needs his clothes washed and ironed. I can simply do some laundry for anyone in exchange for cash, before spending the cash to buy the computer. The money facilitates that chain of transactions.

We can think of the circulation of paper money as a way of keeping track of contributions to society that somebody, somewhere has found valuable. When I did the laundry I made a valuable contribution, and the cash I received was a formal record of that. When I bought the computer, I redeemed my contribution and surrendered the cash. In principle, such transactions could all be recorded on a gigantic centralised database. That's what happens on Yap – the population is small enough that the giant database, keeping track of who owns which stones, can be in their heads. Paper money made that database unnecessary in societies that were too big to use the Yap system, but is increasingly giving way to a giant database as we use debit cards and internet banking more than notes and coins – a computerised version of the Yap islanders' collective memory.

The second function of money is to store value. A dairy farmer hoping to save for retirement cannot just put churns of milk in his basement: the milk is unlikely to retain its value long enough to be of much use. But if the farmer sells the milk for cash, he can certainly put the cash under his mattress – or in a bank account – and store value in that way.

There's a connection between money's functions as a medium of exchange and as a store of value. The medium of exchange allows us to move purchasing power through space – from one situation (doing the laundry) to another (buying a computer). The store of value moves purchasing power through time. Still, good stores of value are not necessarily good media of exchange, and vice versa. A house can be an excellent store of value, but anyone who has ever tried to buy and sell property can attest that it's a lousy medium of exchange. The *rai* of Yap were a very good store of value, but the medium of exchange wasn't the stones themselves, it was the Yap society's mental book-keeping.

The final function of money is in some ways the most important, and the strangest. Money is a unit of account. An alternative way to phrase that is to say that money is a kind of reference point, a standard of value. Let's reach for another analogy with mass. I could tell you that I weigh 88 kilograms, or 194 pounds, or 176 bags of sugar. You might think it doesn't matter which way I choose to express it, right?

Of course. Whichever way you say it, you still weigh just the same.

I used to think that, too. But I've come to realise that the unit of account does sometimes matter; my undergraduate tutor, Anthony Courakis, took great pains to persuade me of this. Imagine you did have a million dollars' worth of financial assets – a pile of bonds, shares and various currencies with a total value of a million bucks.

Lucky me.

Indeed. Now, at the time of writing you could call that £641,500, or €795,800. Or you could call it 10,893 barrels of oil. Or 1730 shares in Apple. Of course, none of those descriptions are literally true: you don't literally have 1730 shares in Apple, and you don't literally have a heap of a million dollars, you have a whole load of different assets with that total value. The question is, what would be the most helpful way to think about your net worth?

The answer is that the most valuable way of tracking your net worth is to find out what unit of account is stable relative to the kind of things you want to buy. If you plan to retire to Florida then it's probably helpful to think of yourself as a dollar millionaire. If you want to buy a house in Edinburgh, it would be more helpful to think of yourself as a sterling six-hundred-and-forty-one-thousand-aire. If your plans involve digging a giant hole and pouring Brent Crude into it, then it might be helpful to think of yourself as an oil ten-thousand-barrel-aire; but otherwise, barrels of oil would be unlikely to be a helpful way to think of your net worth. The same goes for Apple shares: over the past year, at the time of writing, your million dollars would have fluctuated between almost 3200 Apple shares and a little over 1500 Apple shares – at all points still being worth a million dollars. Unless your local shops accept payment only in Apple shares, it's probably more helpful to use dollars as your unit of account.

That's what I mean by a standard of value: if you want to keep track of how you are doing, it helps to choose a unit of measurement that is stable relative to the problem at hand. This will often mean thinking of your salary or your net worth in terms of a currency, because good currencies typically are quite stable relative to all the things you might want to buy. It is confusing to think of your salary in terms of Apple shares; for that matter it is confusing to think of your salary in terms of apples.

Over the years, when commodities have been used as money, the fact that they've been stable units of account has been hugely important.

For example, salt was used in early contracts – it's the basis of the word 'salary' and it seems likely that Roman soldiers were originally paid in salt. This makes sense, because salt had a very stable value. The demand for salt is stable, because everybody needs a bit, but nobody wants a lot; the supply of salt, meanwhile, was also stable because it was produced by age-old techniques. If both supply and demand are stable, so is the price – and price stability is just what you need in your unit of account.

But this all seems mind-bogglingly obvious – why on earth *wouldn't* a US citizen think of her salary as dollars rather than jelly beans, or apples, or salt? Or a German citizen think of his salary as euros, not bratwurst?

If it seems completely obvious, it's because the unit-of-account role of money is so basic, so absolutely fundamental, it's hard to think yourself into a scenario where it comes into conscious play. One recent example that made me chuckle was a tweet from James Rickards, an enthusiast for gold and a return to the gold standard. In April 2013, as the price of gold was collapsing, Mr Rickards commented, 'Last week I had x ounces of #Gold. Today

I have x ounces. So value is unchanged. Constant at x ounces. Dollar is volatile though. #ThinkOz'. Now, I don't have a view either way on where the price of gold is going next, but it's pretty clear that this tweet is absurd, and thinking about how money needs to be a good unit of account tells us why. If Mr Rickards wants to buy a hamburger, or a suit, or a car, he'll find that the dollar hasn't been volatile at all: the prices of these things have changed slowly when measured in dollars. They have gyrated wildly when measured in ounces of gold – which is why gold is not money, at least not at the moment. It may be a good investment or a bad investment, but that's a different question.

One could tell a similar story about Bitcoin, a decentralised electronic 'currency'. Bitcoin was developed in 2008 by a mysterious person or group of people with the pseudonym Satoshi Nakamoto. He, she or they developed a way by which Bitcoins could be produced, or mined, slowly – a bit like gold. Some people love Bitcoin for the same reason that some people love gold – it's independent from any government, and there's a hard limit on how many Bitcoins can ever exist. But just like gold, Bitcoin is not money for a very simple reason: it's far too volatile. On 10 April 2013, for instance, the price of Bitcoins dropped by 61 per cent. Again, Bitcoins may prove to be a smart long-term investment. But they aren't money. Maybe that's obvious to you, but there are a lot of gold-and-Bitcoin enthusiasts out there who don't seem to have realised this.

This does suggest, though, that a dollar isn't automatically money either – it's only money if it keeps a reasonably stable value.

Absolutely. When my tutor Tony Courakis was a young boy in post-war Greece, he played Monopoly with real money – German marks and Greek drachma – that had become worthless. When the Greeks wished to agree some long-term contract, they often used the British gold sovereign to denominate the transaction, even though no sovereigns would actually change hands.

Another example is when the dollar wasn't good enough money to use in contracts to pay the soldiers fighting for Massachusetts in the US Revolutionary War. The Continental Congress, the body which issued the Declaration of Independence, was printing money but nobody knew how much it might be worth when the war was over – and indeed it turned out to be worth very little. So Massachusetts promised its soldiers the value of 68 4/7 lb of beef, 16 lb of leather, 5 bushels of corn and 10 lb of sheep's wool at the end of the war.[4] Note that Massachusetts wasn't actually proposing to hand sacks of produce to each soldier – they would be paid in cash. The point was that promises of any specific amount of cash were hard to weigh up. By offering cash to the value of this portfolio of commodities, Massachusetts discovered a way of making that promise comprehensible in a chaotic environment.

More recently, Nico Colchester, a journalist at the *Financial Times*, pointed out that the Mars Bar was a fantastically stable unit of account – a veritable ingot of milk, sugar and cocoa. Colchester showed that all sorts of prices had stayed stable over the decades, provided that the Mars Bar was used as the unit of account.

That's all very interesting, but I'm not planning to have a revolutionary war in my economy any time soon. And I am not aware of any proposals to adopt the Mars Bar as a unit of currency.

The fact that the Mars Bar hasn't caught on is, I think, a great vote of confidence in the stability of modern paper currencies such as the dollar, the pound and the euro. Despite financial chaos, the Mars Bar remains nothing more than a sugary snack, which is surely reassuring.

Now, by the end of the last chapter we'd seen why it can sometimes be a good idea to tackle a recession by firing up the printing presses. I promised you that this discussion of money would help us to understand why it isn't always a good idea to try to solve your economic problems by printing more banknotes.

Let me guess: you're about to use the word 'Zimbabwe'.

That's as good an example as any. It wasn't long ago that Zimbabwe had so much inflation that they had to knock three zeros off the end of their currency, so the billions became millions and the millions became thousands. You might think that would do the trick, but no: they had to knock off another ten zeros shortly afterwards. Cumulatively that revaluation would turn a ten trillion dollar bill into a one dollar bill. Even then, they still had to print notes for a hundred trillion Zimbabwean dollars. If they hadn't revalued, that would have been a sextillion dollar note.

Come on, I want to see that written down. Can I crook my little finger to my mouth like Dr Evil?

If you must. One sextillion Zimbabwean dollars is written Z$1,000,000,000,000,000,000,000, which is a number more than ten million times larger than the world's annual economic output, expressed in US dollars. We economists call this kind of thing hyperinflation, and it makes modern economic life near impossible. Hyperinflation is typically defined as an inflation rate of over 50 per cent a month. Imagine, for instance, borrowing $1 million to buy a house in a country that then starts to experience 50 per cent monthly inflation rates. Before three years are out, a cup of coffee will cost you more than $1 million. Your salary will be measured in billions. The mortgage on your million-dollar home will be laughable, and the person who lent you the money will be cursing the day that she did. Indeed, when hyperinflation takes hold, anybody who had a debt will find that the debt is trifling; anybody who had money in the bank, under a mattress, or loaned (perhaps to the government) will find that their savings are worthless. Pensions, too, will be worthless unless properly linked to keep up with inflation – and when prices are rising so quickly, the slightest slippage with the inflation-linking will doom the pension.

Inflation of 50 per cent a month is spectacular enough, then. But in October 1923 in Germany, monthly inflation was nearly 30,000 per cent, as prices more than doubled every four days. All the clichés were true: people used wheelbarrows to cart the cash around, and they used cigarettes instead of currency, while they used currency instead of firewood. Erich Maria Remarque's novel, *The Black Obelisk*, describes life in this era. After lighting a cigar with a 10 mark bill, the narrator, Ludwig, turns to his friend Georg. 'How are we doing really? Are we ruined or in clover?' Georg replies: 'I don't believe anyone in Germany knows that about himself.' That's hyperinflation: no one knows where they stand.

Although Germany's experience has become infamous, it is dwarfed by more recent episodes: by Yugoslavia in 1994, where monthly inflation topped 300 million per cent; by Zimbabwe in 2008; and in particular by Hungary in 1946. Hungary holds the unenviable world record for the highest ever monthly rate of inflation at 41,900,000,000,000,000 per cent – a rate at which prices more than treble every day, and your monthly salary wouldn't buy a cup of coffee if you waited a week to spend it. (The equivalent annual inflation rate is, if my arithmetic serves, a number with 178 digits.) Not that anyone would receive a monthly salary under such circumstances, for obvious reasons: prices are rising by 5 per cent an hour. If you were thinking of going out for a restaurant meal you'd be smart to eat quickly, or pay in advance.

This all sounds obviously very bad, and it is. But now that we understand something about money, we can specify precisely why it's so bad. Hyperinflation destroys the three things that make for good money. Banknotes cease to be a handy medium of exchange when you have to carry them around in a wheelbarrow. Hyperinflation makes money useless as a store of value, meaning that saving and borrowing become all but impossible. And, as Ludwig and Georg discovered, money becomes useless as a unit of account: it becomes impossible to work out what anyone or anything is worth, without referring to some alternative currency. A few weeks of hyperinflation and you'd find your citizens adopting the Mars Bar as a currency before you could say Fintlewoodlewix.

In the next chapter, we'll put these concepts – medium of exchange, store of value, unit of account – to further use. But to close this chapter, how about another inspiring success story?

I could do with some cheering up.

I thought so. We're going to see how the humble, ethereal 'unit of account' function of money solved a huge problem for one of the world's great emerging markets – Brazil. When the radio show *This American Life* covered the story I'm about to tell, they called it 'the lie that saved Brazil'.[5] I wouldn't put it quite like that.

And how would you put it?

It wasn't a lie. It was more like a ghost currency.

A ghost currency? I rather like that.

The story starts in the 1990s. Brazil had been suffering from bouts of inflation for decades, and prices in the country were increasing by 80 per cent a month – comfortably clearing the hurdle of 50 per cent a month which defines hyperinflation. A loaf of bread costing one cruzeiro in January would cost more than three cruzeiros in March, more than a hundred by

September, and well over a thousand the following January. We saw in the last chapter that it costs money to change prices; in Brazil in the early 1990s, every supermarket employed somebody whose job it was to walk around the store sticking new labels on all the products – with prices rising by about 2 per cent a day, it was pretty much a full-time job. Supermarket customers, meanwhile, had to run around trying to get ahead of him. Life became inconvenient in all kinds of other ways, too. Just received your week's wages? Get it spent, quickly. Agreed a price to sell a house? Fine – but make sure you also agreed *when* the price would be paid. Every day of foot dragging without the price increasing, and the buyer is getting a better deal.

Since Brazilian money was a poor medium of exchange and a worse store of value, it wasn't a terribly impressive kind of money at all. Small wonder that Brazil's politicians tried everything to sit on the inflation problem. President Sarney, in the mid-1980s, made it illegal to raise prices. This is a common response to inflation, and the response was the same in Brazil as it always is: since prices were being kept artificially low, sellers took their products off the shelves until prices increased again. (Beef farmers even hid their cows. As *This American Life* was told: Brazil's a big country. You can hide cows if you need to.) The few sales that did occur were at black-market prices.

Another attempt at a solution was to replace the currency with a new, improved, non-inflationary currency. Brazil's politicians tried this a lot. First the cruzeiro was replaced with the cruzado, in 1986. The next year, the cruzado itself was re-valued. The year after, the cruzado had to be replaced with the new cruzado. Two years after that, the cruzeiro was back; and in 1993, the cruzeiro was replaced again, this time with the cruzero real. Introducing new currencies has sometimes halted inflation, but not this time, and it is hardly surprising that after five new currencies in seven years, people started to doubt that inflation could ever be defeated.[6]

Four academic economists now enter our story: people who had spent their careers studying Brazilian inflation and slapping their foreheads over the idiocy of each new government. These friends, former college drinking pals, were reluctant to get involved in politics. But pretty soon, the politicians were begging. Edmar Bacha, one of the four, was summoned by the President himself, Itamar Franco. When Bacha asked for an autograph for his children, Franco wrote, 'Please tell your father to work fast for the benefit of the country.' He couldn't really refuse.

The new plan relied on separating out the three functions of money. Previous attempts to introduce new currencies had attempted to replace the medium of exchange, store of value and unit of account functions simultaneously, and had all failed in a flurry of cruzeros and cruzados. The new plan was different. Brazil wouldn't introduce a new currency. It would stick with the cruzeiro, however spelled. The medium of exchange would remain the cruzeiro. The store of value, such as it was, would remain the cruzeiro. But the unit of account would change.

How could that work?

It was absurdly simple. Every price in every shop would no longer be listed in cruzeiros but in URV, or *unidade real de valor* ('units of real value'). Your salary would be listed in URV. Everything would be listed in URV. But the URV did not exist; it was a ghost currency. Transactions were settled in cruzeiros. Wallets were stuffed with cruzeiros and so were cash registers. And if you wanted to know how much that loaf of bread was in cruzeiros, simple: the daily exchange rate would be calculated by the central bank each day, published in the newspapers, and might well be listed for convenience on the wall of most shops. This official exchange rate between URVs and cruzeiros was changing every day, because the cruzeiro was worth less and less every day. But the URV? The URV kept its value. (For a while, it was pegged to the US dollar.)

A strange thing started to happen at that point. You'd see that every month you were paid 500 URVs' worth of cruzeiros – that would be more and more cruzeiros each month, of course. And every day you'd go to the store and buy bread. And it would be – for instance – one URV. It was always one URV. No need for the price-label man to run around the supermarket. That one URV would be more cruzeiros each time, naturally, and you'd be paying for the loaf with cruzeiros. But why would you think about the loaf in terms of cruzeiros? It is much more natural to think of the loaf in terms of its price in URVs.

This is the remarkable achievement of the ghost currency: without ever taking any kind of physical form, it became the way in which Brazilians instinctively thought about what things were worth. It became Brazil's unit of account without assuming the other roles of money. It seems like a bizarre psychological conjuring trick, but perhaps the trick was not so hard to pull off. It's not easy to go through life in a modern economy without a unit of account, and a currency that's going through 80 per cent inflation a month isn't much of a unit of account. People's minds were scrabbling about for a foothold in an ever-shifting economic landscape. The URV was that foothold.

This wasn't the only change in policy, of course. The Brazilian government was turning off the printing presses, balancing its budget, clamping down on wage inflation, and so on. The cruzeiro inflation rate was falling. But the key was the psychological fixed point of the URV, which helped everybody figure out what everything was really worth.

One day, 1 July 1994, the Brazilian government simply abolished the cruzeiro and replaced it with the long-stable URV, now called the *real*. The gang of four economists had promised that inflation would end overnight. And it did.

It's encouraging to know that there's a cure for hyperinflation. But I suppose prevention is better than cure.

You suppose right.

Let me recap, then. In Chapter 2, you told me it's sometimes a good idea to print money. In Chapter 3, you've told me it's never a good idea to print too much money. I'm sure you can guess my next question: how much money should I print?

We'll answer that in Chapter 4. But I'll spoil the surprise now, if you like: the amount of money you should print is *just enough*.

4

Just enough inflation

'"Are we ruined or in clover?"

"I don't believe anyone in Germany knows that about himself."'

Erich Maria Remarque, *The Black Obelisk*

'Just enough'? What kind of a smart-aleck answer is that?

It's not as obvious as it sounds, actually. Now that you're in charge of an economy, you'll doubtless have people telling you that you shouldn't be getting involved in the money-printing business at all. These are people who have been so spooked by episodes of hyperinflation, they have concluded that any degree of inflation is to be avoided – for example, by linking your currency to gold.

That would avoid inflation?

Almost inevitably, although rulers have occasionally debased the currency, diluting the link between money and gold. But as long as the link between currency and gold remained strong and true, you'd get inflation only if there were a sudden glut of gold. Even then, the inflation rate would be tiny. For instance, there was a notorious bout of inflation in the century after Christopher Columbus arrived in the Americas, because gold and silver seized by the conquistadors began to pour across the Atlantic from the New World to Europe. In the sixteenth century, prices in Europe roughly doubled – or equivalently, the value of gold and silver roughly halved. It wasn't the first bout of inflation in history – that may have been when Alexander the Great conquered Persia and spent the Persian emperor's gold – but it's famous. It's also pathetic by twentieth-century standards: the annual inflation rate during the sixteenth century was around 0.7 per cent. (There's a handy rule of thumb called the 'rule of 72' – divide 72 by the annual inflation rate and the result is approximately how many years it will take prices to double. In this case, 72 divided by 0.7 gives you prices doubling in a century.) Nowadays, 0.7 per cent inflation isn't much: these days central banks aim for 2 per cent inflation, or thereabouts. At that rate, prices would double every thirty-five years or so.

Wait a minute. You're telling me that central banks actually want some inflation? Why don't they aim for zero?

Not only do central banks want inflation, I'm going to argue that they should want even more. But to answer your second question, think back to our discussion of the babysitting co-op and sticky prices. Specifically, remember the money illusion – the professor who was infuriated by a pay cut, but didn't mind a below-inflation pay rise, even though they are exactly the same thing. That should tell you that a little bit of inflation can be quite helpful. Imagine a sector of the economy in which productivity is falling, perhaps because foreign competition is reducing the price that companies can get for their products. Wages need to be trimmed or the whole sector is likely to go bust. We know that bosses probably can't get away with cutting nominal wages. If inflation is zero, that means they won't be able to cut real wages either. But if there's some inflation, they can get away with making the necessary cuts to real wages by giving below-inflation rises.

There's another reason to aim for a bit of inflation, one that's arguably even more important: monetary policy is not a precise science. Central banks will sometimes overshoot and sometimes undershoot their targets. If they aim for zero inflation and undershoot, they get deflation – and I want to persuade you that deflation is a much more serious problem than moderate inflation.

Go on, then.

Deflation, as I'm sure you've guessed, is when prices fall year after year after year.

That doesn't sound too bad.

Doesn't it? Imagine borrowing £300,000 to buy a house, and slowly repaying the money on a monthly basis. Normally, with a small amount of inflation, that monthly repayment would gradually come to represent less and less of a burden. Your salary would be rising; the prices of all the other products you bought would be rising; but the monthly repayment would stay the same in nominal terms and in comparison to everything else, it would be shrinking. No problem.

But with deflation, prices begin to drop. Your wages are a price, so they are falling. Of course, the prices of food, clothes and fuel are all falling, too. But your mortgage repayment never changes. It is taking up a larger and larger portion of your monthly salary. Your loss is some saver's gain, of course. But remember that in a recession, what we want is people spending money to stimulate economic activity. Redistributing money from borrowers to savers is going to achieve the exact opposite, because borrowers are more likely to be spending than savers – they wouldn't be borrowing otherwise. Add in the problem that when lots of people find it hard to pay back their loans, the entire banking system can run into trouble.

That's not the only reason deflation makes it harder to kick-start an economy out of recession. As prices are falling, cash will always buy more tomorrow than it does today – so people will naturally postpone non-essential purchases for as long as they can, depressing demand further. And as banks are unlikely to be offering generous interest rates – because there aren't many people clamouring to borrow money in a deflationary environment – many savers decide to keep their cash in biscuit tins or under mattresses. Once cash is taken out of the banking system, it can't be lent out. The effect of all this? Still less demand and still more deflation, of course.

In a deflationary environment, there are no good options. To the extent that prices are sticky and don't adjust downwards, everything is more expensive than it should be so demand remains depressed; to the extent that prices do adjust downwards, this gives everybody the incentive to postpone spending, so demand remains depressed. You're stuck. This is basically what happened in the Great Depression in the 1930s, and it went on for years.

The most straightforward and direct solution is to expand the money supply. Unfortunately, at the time of the Great Depression, many currencies were still backed by gold. This was a problem, because you can print money, but you can't print gold.

So I should just ignore people who tell me to link my monetary system to gold?

Yes.

Eventually, in the Great Depression, one by one, countries dropped off the gold standard – often with great reluctance. As they left the gold standard, they started printing paper money that was nothing more than paper, and their domestic money supplies expanded. Prices began to rise; real wages fell, and therefore companies started to hire workers again. And one by one, in largely the same order as they had left the gold standard, these economies started to recover.

Your central bank can create money from thin air. It's like a superpower.[1] Use it.

But this is absurd – won't printing billions of dollars create hyperinflation?

You don't mean 'billions', you mean 'trillions'. The US Federal Reserve has created over $2 trillion of new money since the crisis, and has been printing money and buying up bonds at the rate of $40 billion a month, sometimes more. A lot of it is money in bank accounts, not actual printed paper money, but 'printing money' is the simple way to talk about this.

Now some excitable stock-picking commentators have been claiming since this kind of money-printing began, it was just a matter of time before the US turned into Zimbabwe. If hyperinflation didn't strike in 2010, it would strike in 2011. Or in 2012 for sure. And it hasn't.

Not yet, anyway. But why not? $40bn a month sounds like a lot.

It is a lot – over $100 of new money for every US resident, every month. But the reason it doesn't turn into hyperinflation is that there's no simple linear link between the amount of cash in circulation – whether notes, coins, or current account deposits – and the price pressure on an economy. If you print a hundred dollars and give it to a starving man, he'll spend it. If on the other hand you give the $100 to a ninety-year-old lady with a decent pension and an anxious disposition, she may simply put it in a cookie jar, just in case she needs it. That $100 is going to do nothing whatsoever to stimulate demand and it will not increase inflation either. And at the moment, despite enthusi-astic money-printing from many of the world's central banks since 2008, a lot of the money is ending up in the equivalent of cookie jars. The money may be helping prop up spending, or it may be distorting decisions and storing up trouble for the future. But one thing it is not doing is creating hyperinflation: inflation remains close to the central bankers' targets.

This is making me nervous. I can see that if I target 2 per cent, I can undershoot by 2 per cent without triggering deflation. But presumably I'm just as likely to overshoot by 2 per cent, and end up with 4 per cent inflation. According to your rule of 72, that would double prices in less than two decades. Isn't that a problem?

Not obviously.

Don't forget that when inflation is 4 per cent, you'll typi-cally be able to get an interest rate on savings accounts which preserves the value of your savings – or, at the very least, sig-nificantly slows the rate at which it erodes. I know that as I write, inflation in many developed countries is positive yet interest rates are close to zero. But that's very unusual and it's the financial crisis that's to blame. In more normal times, when inflation is low, interest rates will be low, and when inflation is a little bit higher, interest rates will be, too.

Then there are salaries: they usually rise in line with infla-tion. The same is true for pensions. There are exceptions, of course – that's what sticky prices are all about. But we can gen-erally assume that when prices are rising by 4 per cent then nominal wages, pensions and income from savings will not be too far behind. And while 4 per cent inflation doubles the price of everything in less than twenty years, if wages also roughly double, who cares?

I can give you practical examples of countries with non-trivial inflation yet strong economic growth: India and China. A generation ago, China had two nasty bouts of inflation, with prices increasing by over 25 per cent a year. That had serious political consequences: the inflation of the late 1980s (and government attempts to stop it) were contributors to the famous, violently suppressed Tiananmen Square protests of 1989. But the economy coped just fine – China's rapid growth quickly erased whatever economic consequences there were. India, like China, has had some inflationary episodes. But despite average inflation of around 5–8 per cent for both countries over the past twenty-five years, well above what a rich country's central bank would aim for, India and China have both grown strongly. Lower inflation might have been preferable but high inflation has evidently been manageable.

To see why inflation of 4 or 5 per cent is survivable, let's think back to the three functions of money. First, money is a medium of exchange, a way of avoiding the need to barter all the time. Does inflation of 4 per cent a year make a currency a bad medium of exchange? Hardly. We're a long way from needing wheelbarrows to carry our banknotes around.

Second, money is a store of value. It allows a farmer to take the income he receives from his crops over the course of a few days a year, and spread out the spending power. It allows a young couple to save for a summer holiday. It also allows working people to save for retirement. Does inflation of 4 per cent a year undermine money's capacity to be a store of value? Yes, to some extent. It wouldn't put me off saving cash in a biscuit tin ahead of my summer holiday, but it would certainly put me off planning for retirement by keeping cash under my mattress. Nonetheless, if there's a reasonably well-functioning financial system, it's not an overwhelming problem, because banks and other financial institutions will help savers seeking a store of value to find borrowers who are eager for cash now. If the interest rate on my savings account is 5 or 6 per cent, inflation of 4 per cent isn't going to make it too challenging for me to use money as a store of value.

Third, money is a unit of account. As we've seen, this is a more profound role for money than it might at first appear. Hyperinflation utterly destroys a currency's role as a unit of account. But, again, inflation of 4 per cent a year typically does not.

What does it mean for a currency to no longer be useful as a unit of account? Let me give an example. I recently went for a drink with a colleague at a fancy West London wine bar; I was charged almost £10 for two beers. For a moment, I was confused. I'm a family man these days: if I have a beer, it will usually be at home; if I go out, it will usually be with my wife to a restaurant. So I wasn't totally familiar with beer prices. The drinks seemed expensive. Had I simply lost track of the price of a beer in London? Or had I walked into the wrong bar? Perhaps the truth was a bit of both. The value of the pound in my pocket had become slightly fuzzy: I couldn't distinguish between a local price increase ('this place is a rip-off') and global inflation ('money was worth something when I was a lad'). But the truth is that this was an unusual example –

because most of what we buy, we buy frequently enough to observe gradual price increases – and a trivial one. I don't think I'll go back to the same place, and if I blamed the wine bar for what was really a general rise in inflation, what harm?

There's no real reason to think that moderate inflation – 4 or 5 per cent – destroys the qualities we need for a currency to be useful money.

Hmm. 'Moderate inflation' sounds a bit like 'moderate pregnancy' to me. How do I know that my 4 per cent a year isn't going to inch upwards and upwards until it's 50 per cent a month and we've got hyperinflation on our hands?

I applaud your concern. The first thing to say in response is that the historical record is quite reassuring.[2] A recent attempt to categorise every episode of hyperinflation in history produced a list of fifty-six – and Iran in late 2012 is the fifty-seventh. Three-quarters of these hyperinflations occurred in one of three clear clusters: central European states after the First World War, including the most famous hyperinflation in history, Weimar Germany; during or immediately after the Second World War, including Hungary, history's worst; and Eastern Bloc countries as the Soviet Union disintegrated, comprising over half of all the twentieth century's hyper-inflations. These are all examples of hyperinflation following some extreme stress on the political and social system. Most of the remaining examples, from Zimbabwe to sanction-struck Iran to late revolutionary France, are also associated with some exceptional political crisis, even humanitarian disaster.

Yes, but is the hyperinflation the consequence of the disaster – or does it cause the problems?

The disaster comes first and the hyperinflation follows, making things worse. Hyperinflation in Germany in 1923 didn't cause the First World War. Hyperinflation in Iran didn't cause sanctions.

Typically, hyperinflation begins because the authorities don't have enough money to respond to an unusual situation – say, to pay for a war, or keep paying civil servants' salaries during a social and economic upheaval that makes it hard to collect enough taxes – so they see no option but to print money and keep on printing. The trouble is that while governments can create money out of thin air, getting people to accept the money as payment for their services is another matter altogether. As the printing presses churn out more and more money with no end in sight, the amount of cash chasing any particular product on the shelf will rise and rise. So will prices, inevitably, and then a self-reinforcing spiral sets in: people naturally expect prices to increase further and further, so they demand ever higher wages. Pretty soon, the situation is out of control. Not only do prices keep rising but the rate at which they keep rising is also going up – inflation accelerates.

In principle, certainly, a similar 'wage–price spiral' can take hold at moderate levels of inflation in an economy which hasn't just experienced a hugely stressful event such as a war or a revolution. But history shows that it doesn't tend to happen. Some wealthy countries experienced what looks like a wage–price spiral in the 1970s, where a combination of oil price increases and relaxed monetary policy led to annual inflation in double digits, sometimes even more than 20 per cent. But 20 per cent annual inflation isn't 50 per cent monthly inflation. It's not even close. And in the end, central banks did manage to prevent this spiral from turning into hyperinflation.

Ultimately, like any self-respecting superhero, you simply have to realise that with great power comes great responsibility. You have to know when to stop.

Like you need to stop drinking after a couple of beers, you mean.

Just so: an occasional drink can kick-start a dull evening, but drinking constantly is not a good idea. William McChesney Martin, the Chairman of the Federal Reserve throughout the 1950s and 1960s, explained that his job was 'to take away the punch bowl just as the party gets going'. Not only does a party host not want things to get out of hand, but the host must also think ahead, because alcohol has a delayed effect. By the time people are visibly drunk, they probably have a couple of extra drinks in their stomach just waiting to make their presence felt. Similarly for monetary policy: everything takes place after a delay.

I have occasionally been known to misjudge my beer intake, it's true. Are there any tell-tale warning signs I should be looking out for that I'm printing too much money?

There are a couple, though – unfortunately – neither is very black-and-white.

The first warning sign is that people start to become quite conscious of inflation when they make decisions. As we've seen, a little bit of inflation is helpful, in part, precisely because people don't tend to think very clearly about it – like our economics professor offered a 3 per cent pay rise at a time of 6 per cent inflation – which makes it easier for some real prices to undergo a downward adjustment when needed. If inflation climbs to, say, 25 per cent a year, however, most people will explicitly consider it in their daily affairs, because it is just too costly to ignore it. They will start to write it into contracts, imposing additional costs on doing business – and as they factor expectations of inflation into their thinking, it makes your job of reducing inflation all the harder.

The second warning sign is what some economists call 'malinvestment'. To see what this is, remember that even the keenest proponents of printing money acknowledge that it has limits. Ultimately, any particular economy at a particular time has a finite capacity to produce goods and services. There are only so many factories, only so many hours in the day, and new technology can be introduced only at a certain rate. The idea of printing money is to get the economy functioning at or near its capacity. But if the economy is already at the limits of its capacity to supply, where will that extra money you're printing end up going? Without sensible opportunities to invest the new cash, people will start buying investment assets such as dot-com shares, Shanghai condominiums, or bonds backed by repackaged sub-prime mortgages. This malinvestment looks profitable at first, because the prices of the assets rise, but ultimately the bubble bursts and the economy is damaged.

The trouble is that it isn't always obvious when malinvestment is happening. Think of the impact of Alan Greenspan, Chairman of the US Federal Reserve from the mid-1980s to the mid-2000s. Mr Greenspan used monetary policy to cut interest rates whenever trouble seemed to be threatening an economy. This fuelled a series of bubbles, from the dot-com years, to sub-prime housing, and finally to the credit bubble that so damaged the world economy. The tricky thing is that inflation was always moderate under Alan Greenspan: as a result, there was no consensus at the time that his monetary policy really was too loose, and even in hindsight it is impossible to be sure.

So you've scared me with deflation, and now you're making me nervous about letting inflation creep too high. I still don't understand why two beers – sorry, 2 per cent – is the magic number to aim for. Why not an inflation target of 1 per cent, or 4 per cent?

This is now an active area of debate. The chief economist of the International Monetary Fund (IMF), Olivier Blanchard – also a leading academic – floated the idea of a 4 per cent inflation target in 2010. A raft of other top academics from both ends of the political spectrum were also making the case for a higher inflation target, from Greg Mankiw (Harvard professor, textbook author, senior advisor to George W. Bush) to Paul Krugman (Princeton professor, Nobel laureate, tormentor of Republicans everywhere).

There is one straightforward reason to suspect that a higher target might be a good idea: it makes deflation less likely, which is sensible because deflation is dangerous and hard to cure.

Other reasons are more of a mixed blessing. Inflation of 4 per cent might help prices adjust more sensibly than a 2 per cent target – in particular, when real wages need to fall but nominal wages stubbornly stay put, higher inflation will allow real wages to fall more quickly. This is true, but there's a countervailing point: in a world where prices tend to stick awkwardly, higher underlying inflation will create distortions. Imagine, for the sake of argument, a menu that can be reprinted only every three years. With 2 per cent underlying inflation, menu prices will be off their initial prices by 6 per cent before they can be reprinted; with inflation at 4 per cent, that distortion will obviously be twice as large. Whether the inflation target should be higher or lower is a question of balance.

Another double-edged argument for higher inflation is that it makes debts melt away. There's little doubt that in the wake of the financial crisis high debt burdens were causing a problem. An economic goddess who waved her magic wand and forgave a chunk of the debt would have helped the economy to grow again, because the debtors who gained were more likely to spend spare cash than the creditors who lost out. A burst of surprise inflation would have achieved much the same as the goddess's magic wand. There are two problems with this argument, though. First, it's hardly fair to make creditors suffer – such as, for example, those saving for pensions – for the convenience of everyone else. And second, it doesn't take much of this sort of thing before future creditors will demand higher interest rates and future borrowers will suffer.

You're sitting on the fence. I hope it's comfortable.

I'm just trying to explain both sides of the argument, because this really is a balancing act. And before I tell you what I think you should do, you could also consider nominal GDP targeting.

Is that a thing?

Yes. Forgive the jargon: nominal GDP targeting is something that's a hot topic in economics at the moment. Here's the basic idea. Imagine that your economy grows at 3 per cent a year on average, with an inflation target of 2 per cent. That implies 'nominal' GDP growth of 5 per cent a year – 3 percentage points are genuine growth and a further 2 percentage points are inflation. So you could set a target of 5 per cent growth in nominal GDP, or NDGP, instead of aiming at 2 per cent inflation.

I get the idea but I don't get the point. Why set a target for nominal GDP growth instead of inflation?

The central bank can affect inflation pretty directly but only indirectly influences real GDP growth, so an NGDP target is really just an inflation target that keeps moving up and down. When real growth is slow, the central bank aims for more inflation and prints extra money. When the economy is growing quickly, the central bank tightens things up. (There are other ways to play this game but you get the picture.) The thinking is that an NGDP target gives us the benefits of a high inflation target when we really need it, but on average inflation should be 2 per cent, as we originally intended.

That sounds pretty clever. Why don't I do that?

Well, it's your economy and you can do it if you like. But I worry that it is slightly too clever for its own good. In theory it's brilliant. In practice you have two serious problems: the public will have absolutely no idea what the central bank is trying to do, and the implicit inflation target will always be moving, which will make it tough for people to plan their financial affairs.

Hmm. Off the fence with you, then – how much inflation is 'just enough'?

I think you should raise the inflation target to 3 per cent or perhaps even 4 per cent. There's a risk in that, of course. Your central bank has worked hard to acquire credibility as a tough-minded inflation-fighter, and that credibility is important to all of us. A new inflation target – or even a totally new system, such as NGDP targeting – might upset the economic apple-cart. The status quo is attractive.

But you're a new broom. Be bold. The costs and benefits of

a 4 per cent inflation target that I laid out a moment ago – in particular, more price distortions but easier wage adjustment – pretty much balance each other out. When you actually look seriously at the costs of inflation at 4 per cent rather than 2 per cent, it's not easy to find anything major.

In my view the clinching argument for a higher inflation target is the one which originally motivated the chief economist of the IMF to take the extraordinary step of proposing such a radical idea. It is that an inflation target of 4 per cent might help you avoid a pernicious economic trap.

A trap?

Imagine a recession during which nominal interest rates fall to zero, or near zero. On second thoughts, don't imagine it, just look around. At the time of writing, this description applies to the United States, the United Kingdom, Japan and the Eurozone. If your own economy has escaped, count yourself lucky.

In this not-nearly-hypothetical-enough situation, how can the central bank stimulate the economy further? One thing that cannot be done is to reduce nominal interest rates: zero is as low as they will go. The reason is obvious. Very few people would put money in a bank, or otherwise lend out money, at an interest rate of minus 1 per cent, because cash under the mattress pays a better rate of interest, namely zero. There's a well-regarded rule of thumb for central bankers that specifies how interest rates should be changed in response to inflation and GDP trends; it suggests that nominal interest rates should have been at minus 2 per cent during the depths of the crisis. Obviously, they weren't. They couldn't have been. That means that too many people were saving money, not enough people were spending it, and the economy was slower to recover than it should have been.

Now if the central bank can't encourage a consumer or investment boom by driving nominal interest rates lower, it could in principle drive real interest rates lower by creating inflation. If inflation is 2 per cent then the lowest possible real interest rate is minus 2 per cent, which sounds low but might not be nearly low enough in a serious recession. If inflation is higher then real interest rates can fall lower. The higher inflation is, the lower 'zero' really is. But if the economy is already in a slump, it might be difficult to create inflation, which is why starting from a higher rate of inflation is helpful.

Why? Can't I just print money and create inflation whenever I want?

Printing money creates inflation only if people want to spend the money right away. And perhaps they don't. After all, interest rates are already zero: if people wanted to spend money, they could already borrow it for nothing. Perhaps, instead of spending it, they will be like the anxious ninety-year-old we imagined earlier and stick it in a cookie jar. It's a recession, after all – you never know when that cash might come in handy.

If this caution is holding people back from spending, the central bank could print vast amounts of cash without creating any inflationary pressure at all – a situation called a 'liquidity trap'. It describes what was going on in the early years of the Great Depression. For decades it was regarded as a curiosity. But the liquidity trap is an active area of research once again – and no wonder.

In theory, a sufficiently determined central bank should be able to break out of a liquidity trap by making people expect future inflation. The central bank effectively wants to say, 'Once we get out of this liquidity trap, you'd better believe that prices are going to rise and the money in your pocket is going to be worth less.' This would help because the fear of future inflation will encourage people to spend money now before its value melts away.

But central banks have been reluctant to make such bold statements. In 2002, faced with hints that deflation was a possibility, Ben Bernanke (then merely a governor at the Federal Reserve) gave a speech announcing that in the unlikely event that deflation took hold, 'we can take comfort that the logic of the printing press example must assert itself'. Print enough money, in other words, and the deflation will end.

But when Mr Bernanke then took over the top job at the Fed and faced a liquidity trap for real, he hesitated. It's easy to talk of 'the printing press' when everything is hypothetical, less easy when you are the boss. It wasn't until September 2012 that the Federal Reserve released a statement announcing open-ended money-printing and explaining that even after economic recovery took hold, monetary policy would be 'highly accommodative' – in other words, interest rates would be very low. The Federal Reserve finally tried to promise future inflation, but it sounded tame and bureaucratic.

Mr Bernanke's protestations remind me of a soft-hearted

parent trying to discipline a naughty child in a public place: 'You'd better behave yourself, because when we get home, it will be straight to bed with no supper! No, it really will. This is your last warning! I'm not going to tell you again! I mean it! Not joking!'

And of course the child never takes the soft parent seriously and supper will, in due course, be served. Poor Mr Bernanke's promise of high inflation later is very similar: 'You'd better spend some money now because when we get out of this liquidity trap I'm going to create some inflation. I mean it! I really will! Last warning! Not joking!'

We have to sympathise: it's easy to see why central bankers struggle to make the threat of inflation sound credible – they've devoted their careers to making exactly the opposite promise. The Federal Reserve spent decades – including some very hard years under Paul Volcker – acquiring a reputation for waging a ruthless, unending war against inflation. That reputation is so powerful and so valuable that people naturally wonder whether the Federal Reserve really would encourage inflation once the slump ended. The trouble is that if people don't believe that threat, they won't start spending and the slump will continue. This is why economists such as the IMF's Olivier Blanchard have concluded that central banks should have been aiming for a bit more inflation all along.

What can I do, then, if my economy is stuck in a liquidity trap?

Better not to get into the trap at all – that's why the 4 per cent inflation target would have helped a lot. Adopt it and it will help you next time – admittedly, 'next time' will hopefully be many decades away. As for today's liquidity trap, perhaps it's time to turn your attention away from the printing presses and towards the policy most firmly associated with John Maynard Keynes: fiscal stimulus.

5

Stimulus

'If the Treasury were to fill old bottles with banknotes, bury them at suitable depths in disused coalmines which are then filled up to the surface with town rubbish, and leave it to private enterprise on well-tried principles of laissez-faire to dig the notes up again ... there need be no more unemployment and, with the help of the repercussions, the real income of the community, and its capital wealth also, would probably become a good deal greater than it actually is.'

John Maynard Keynes,
The General Theory of Employment, Interest and Money

Did he actually say that? (You see? I told you I'm reading those chapter-opening quotes.)

He did, or at least he wrote it. John Maynard Keynes suggested that you could not only boost employment in your economy, but even boost income and wealth, by printing money and burying it.

I thought we were supposed to be getting away from the idea of printing money.

Fair enough. Keynes was making a point by proposing an obviously absurd idea, so in the same spirit let's find an equally ridiculous one that doesn't involve printing new money. Let's say instead that your government finds a warehouse full of stale chocolate coins, the leftovers of some Christmas binge in the mid-1990s. (Fresh chocolate would never do: making new chocolate coins might accidentally stimulate the sugar, cocoa, dairy and gold-coloured foil industries, and we want our example to be as pointless as possible.) You then hire a small army of people to bury the stale chocolate coins at the bottom of disused mineshafts, and then another small army of people to dig the chocolate coins up again. Think of it as Sisyphus meets Willy Wonka.

Right. And why would we do this, exactly?

Well, you wouldn't, obviously. You might well decide that your government should try to boost the economy by hiring a small army of people. But clearly you'd be insane to make them bury and dig up chocolate coins. No, you'd put them to work on mundane and sensible-sounding things like sweeping the streets, or policing the streets, or building new streets, wouldn't you?

I guess so. Or building houses. Or updating the subway system. Come to think of it, perhaps laying superfast broadband to rural areas would be a better use of their time. They could work in early-years education, improving childhood outcomes and freeing parents to join the labour market. Or we could put them to work on green energy infrastructure. So many possibilities. What would you advise?

You see, you're illustrating one of the reasons Keynes chose such an odd example. Because you're a sensible person, you would focus on the microeconomics of the projects in question, which means asking annoyingly reasonable questions such as, 'What are the benefits of having the streets swept?', 'Are the street sweepers doing the job properly?' and, 'Could we do better by outsourcing the job, using taxpayers' money to pay a private-sector firm?' Perhaps you should even stop altogether, trusting that if private citizens want clean streets they will organise themselves to achieve that goal.

All these are perfectly good microeconomic questions to ask of government projects. But government spending has a macroeconomic aspect too. Perhaps Keynes was worried that whenever we consider a project with macroeconomic implications, we distract ourselves with the detail. (Is this *really* the best way to keep the streets clean? Would we rather have rural broadband or an upgraded underground system?) And so we end up rejecting projects because of their doubtful microeconomic benefits, even if the macroeconomics looks good.

It helps us to focus on the macroeconomic case for government spending if we consider a policy that quite obviously has no other benefits whatsoever – like burying and digging up chocolate coins. (Incidentally, Keynes had another reason to talk about buried banknotes; he also wanted to draw an analogy with mining for gold and silver. But fortunately, unlike Keynes, we don't need to get into arguments about a gold standard.)

Of course it would be better to build houses or underground systems, but for now let's follow Keynes and pick a daft project so that we can think more clearly about what government spending of any kind might do for – or to – your economy. So what happens if your government spends, say, a million pounds hiring people to do something completely, idiotically pointless?

My opinion poll ratings go down, I presume.

There is that. But let's stick to the macroeconomic effects. Economists find this question so intriguing that they have a special piece of horrible jargon for it: the 'spending multiplier'.

Here's what the spending multiplier means. If your government spends a million pounds, and the economy grows by a million pounds as a result, the multiplier is one. If you spend a million pounds and the economy doesn't grow at all, the multiplier is zero. If the economy grows by £500,000 due to the extra spending, the multiplier is 0.5. You get the idea. The multiplier can be negative – say you spend a million pounds and the economy shrinks by £200,000 as a result. That's a multiplier of minus 0.2. And it can be bigger than one. If you have a multiplier of 1.6, then for every million pounds you spend, you will find that GDP grows by £1.6m.

Let's start by thinking about a couple of simple cases to illustrate. If you were to implement your chocolate coins policy when your economy was doing well, you'd have a spending multiplier of zero. Your economy is limited by supply constraints: the stock of equipment, the infrastructure available, the workforce, its skills, and the number of hours in the day. If you hire people to bury and exhume chocolate coins, that can only mean they are not available to install kitchens, do waitressing or sell insurance. As the part of the economy controlled by your government expands, the private sector must shrink to accommodate it. Perhaps this is because taxes go up and people spend less money on kitchens. Perhaps it is because your chocolate coin programme drives up wages, making it too expensive for the insurance company to hire agents, and it goes out of business. Whatever the reason, we know – because the economy is not in a slump – that a new government spending programme will not make the economy any bigger. That's what a spending multiplier of zero means – every pound spent by the government grows the economy by zero pounds.

I should point out that this doesn't mean all government spending in a booming economy is a terrible idea. It simply means that we need to apply a cost–benefit test to your spending priorities. And in fact a traditional cost–benefit test of a government policy – such as, 'Is burying and un-burying stale chocolate money really the best thing we can think to do with a million pounds?' – does assume a multiplier of zero. A million-pound spending programme, by definition, increases the size of the government sector by a million pounds, so a multiplier of zero would mean that the private sector would have to shrink by a million pounds if the economy as a whole stays the same size. That's what it really means to say that a project costs the country a million pounds. We should take the policy on its own merits rather than hoping it will produce some fuzzy benefit for the wider economy. And if the policy is chocolate coin burial, the cost–benefit test will not be passed. But if it's road building or staffing hospitals then those policies might well pass a cost–benefit test. They would be worth doing even with a multiplier of zero.

Now let's imagine that we're in a slump, like the Great Depression – which prompted Keynes to write his *General Theory* – or like the recent financial crisis, which led a lot of governments to implement stimulus programmes. Lots of people are unemployed because of sticky wages or sticky prices. People are saving their money rather than spending it, and the savings are sitting in ninety-year-olds' biscuit tins or under mattresses rather than funding physical investment in new roads or factories. Here, supply isn't the limit on economic output; demand is. That means it's perfectly possible for your government spending programme to hire people without hiring them away from the private sector. Imagine that you do so: you spend a million pounds hiring chocolate coin extractors, but the private sector doesn't shrink at all. In this case, every pound you spend makes the economy itself a pound bigger. In the jargon, the spending multiplier is one. The chocolate coin programme is effectively free, and the only cost–benefit question to ask is whether, given a million pounds of free government spending, chocolate coin recycling is the best use of the freebie.

Hold on a moment. If we're not printing money, that million pounds has to come from somewhere. If I raise taxes by a million pounds to pay for my chocolate coin programme, isn't that going to depress the economy just as much as the government spending stimulates it?

Let's not be hasty. Your government is spending a million pounds more, but are the public spending a million pounds less? Not necessarily. Think about how you might respond to getting a higher tax demand than you'd expected. You might meet it by cutting back your spending – perhaps by cancelling a weekend away that you'd planned. Or you might instead decide to raid your savings or turn to your credit card, so that you can go on the weekend away anyway. Instead of taking the hit immediately, you'd cut your spending over a much longer period as you paid off your credit card bill, or rebuilt your savings. And getting people to borrow or raid their savings right now is, of course, precisely what we're trying to achieve to kickstart the economy.

Economists have a fancy term for this kind of thing – consumption smoothing. In one of my first jobs, for example, I was lucky enough to get a signing-on bonus. I didn't immediately go out and spend it, I put it in a savings account. Then, later, I left that job, and while I was out of work, I didn't immediately move back in with my dad; instead, I spent some of those savings to cover my rent while I looked for another job. That's consumption smoothing. Not everyone will want to smooth their consumption, and some people who want to won't be able to because they have no savings and no overdraft or credit card – but many people can and do. For most of us, it's common sense. That means that if government spends an extra million pounds, and takes an extra million pounds in tax, citizens may not reduce their spending by the full million.

In reality, you won't see governments increasing taxes to fund their stimulus programmes. You'll see them borrow the money instead, and that will make the multiplier larger.

Why?

In theory, it shouldn't make any difference. Your taxpayers should think to themselves: 'It's nice that the government hasn't raised taxes now to pay for all this spending. But taxes will have to go up later, and because of interest payments, the eventual tax bill will be larger. I would be well advised to put some money aside now in anticipation of that tax bill.' If that happens, then funding the spending by borrowing instead of by raising taxes will make no difference to anyone. But this is not, of course, what happens in practice – citizens won't put aside the full amount to pay for future taxes, so you will tend to get a higher multiplier from your spending if you finance it through borrowing than if you insist on raising taxes to balance your budget.

But if I borrow the million pounds, won't that drive up interest rates, encouraging people to put off their own spending till later?

If the economy's doing well, then yes, it would. But remember we're assuming that this chocolate coin programme is happening in an economy that's in a terrible slump. In a slump, people aren't keen to borrow. And if you're not competing with other potential borrowers, then it's perfectly possible that you could borrow money for your stimulus programme without forcing up interest rates.

Ever heard the phrase 'there's no such thing as a free lunch'? What you're describing sounds very much like a free lunch.

That's exactly what we're talking about. When Barack Obama's Council of Economic Advisers estimated the multiplier effect of the 2009 stimulus bill, for example, they were working with multipliers as high at 1.6. In other words, they anticipated that for every million dollars the government borrowed and spent, the US economy would grow by $1.6 million.

A multiplier of 1.6 is possible because each pound you spend hiring chocolate coin workers could, in principle, circulate through multiple transactions, each one of them counting towards GDP. So, for example, one of your newly employed chocolate coin miners – we'll call her Annie – gets her first week's pay, of £100. She takes her family out to a local restaurant to celebrate. The next day, the restaurant owner, call him Bill, uses the £100 to buy a long-coveted painting from Charlie's art gallery. Charlie uses that £100 to pay Diana to fix his leaky roof. And so on.

Come on. There's got to be some kind of catch.

OK, there is a catch. In fact, there are three. We've already met the first one: you'd better be sure that your economy really is in a slump when you implement your chocolate coin programme. When your government spends money to try to give the economy a boost, the economy itself can push back. One way is through the financial system: as you spend money, interest rates will tend to rise, which as you said yourself, will encourage people to delay their own spending. The second way is through a hard limit on what the economy can supply: if you hire good people away from the private sector, burn fuel that was needed elsewhere, rent office space that others wanted, then the result will not be an increase in the economy's real productive output. It will merely be inflation.

To get a high multiplier, you need to assume that this economic counterthrust doesn't happen. Interest rates are zero and do not rise. Hordes of workers are unemployed, machinery lies idle and buildings are empty. Your chocolate coin mines merely shorten the lines for the dole. The increase in production isn't inflationary – it's perfectly real. In such circumstances the multiplier can be very large. But only in such circumstances.

The second catch is that, if you spend your stimulus money in the wrong place, the eventual multiplier could be less than zero. Suppose you raise a million pounds in taxes, and spend the money entirely on buying fine French wine for the government wine cellar – it is thirsty work running the country, after all. Your citizens have responded to the million-pound tax rise by spending less – and you've spent their million pounds in France, boosting the French economy, and shrinking your own. The multiplier is negative. So buy domestic products.

I thought you economists were all in favour of free trade.

We are big fans of free trade, as that's usually the way to get the cheapest, highest-quality products. But we're assuming very special circumstances here: the economy is stuck in a recession thanks to lack of demand and the government is trying to stimulate it. In those circumstances, discriminating against foreign products makes sense for the whole economy.

You said there were three catches. What's the third one?

We've been talking about a one-off programme. You raise a million pounds by taxing or borrowing, you spend the million pounds, and – boom – your economy gets a much-needed shot of adrenaline. But it's in the nature of government projects that they tend to create vested interests with a strong incentive to keep the cash flowing indefinitely. Before you know it, you have the Union of Cocoa Entombers and Exhumers hiring lobbyists, you have elected representatives in constituencies with disused mineshafts calling for the programme to be expanded, you have the civil servants who've been put in charge of the programme doing everything they can to safeguard their jobs, and so on. It might be a case of 'act in haste, repent at leisure'.

What if I borrowed £1 million and used it to cut income tax, rather than fund government spending? That would avoid the 'repent at leisure' problem, wouldn't it?

You might still find it hard to put that tax back up again. But in general, there's a reason why it's more effective to stimulate the economy through government spending than by giving people a tax rebate – some of those tax rebates will go straight into savings accounts, or be spent on imports, neither of which will directly boost the economy. The point of stimulus is that the money should be spent, and the best way to guarantee that is to spend it yourself.

On the other hand, tax cuts do have the advantage of being very quick to implement, whereas it might take you months to organise the logistics of burying chocolate coins. And if you cut sales tax or VAT rather than income tax, then that will have a more direct effect of encouraging spending. Still, in theory, if you want to make sure money is spent boosting an economy, the best way is to spend it yourself.

Enough of the theory. Before I hire my army of chocolate coin workers, I want to be able to tell in advance what it's going to do to my economy. Will the multiplier be negative, zero, one, 1.6? What's the real-world evidence?

That's a slightly sensitive question, I'm afraid. I am all in favour of using as much empirical evidence as possible, but when it comes to the multiplier, this is no easy task – in any complex economy, there's just too much going on.

For the sake of being specific, think about the United States. Stimulus attempts began during the presidency of George W. Bush, with a tax rebate for most taxpayers that had a total value of around $100 billion during 2008. After President Obama's election, a further $800 billion stimulus was passed early in 2009. Almost $300 billion of this was in the form of tax rebates and other tax cuts. Other chunks – for instance, $100 billion of infrastructure funding – weren't necessarily spent in 2009. Still other chunks – such as the $50 billion of aid to school districts – were designed to offset spending cuts at a more local level, so they weren't really 'stimulus' but 'anti-anti-stimulus'. Then there was the notorious 'cash for clunkers' programme: for one month during the summer of 2009, the government gave people an incentive – around $4000 – to scrap old cars and replace them with new, more efficient vehicles. Monetary policy was very loose at the time, with the Federal Reserve printing money, cutting interest rates and providing plenty of support for struggling banks and insurance companies. US export markets were weak. As I say, there was a lot going on. So was the stimulus too big? Too small? Spent at the right time or the wrong time? Likely to increase spending, or directed at other priorities? In the alternative universe in which no stimulus occurred, what would have happened? We can try to look at the path of unemployment and economic growth and compare it to the injection of stimulus; but any conclusions have to be pretty tentative. You can tell a similar story for the United Kingdom, Brazil, China, France, Greece, Iceland, Ireland, Italy, Japan, Spain and a host of other countries that responded to the financial crisis with a smorgasbord of initiatives and against a backdrop of global economic fluctuations. With the best of intentions it is hard to be sure which policies had which effects.

Some credible studies after the US stimulus reckoned the multiplier for the most successful bits of the stimulus (payments to low-income households and to state governments) was around two, which is impressive. But other studies were much more sceptical.[1] And some parts of the stimulus were roundly criticised. For example, an evaluation of the cash for clunkers programme by Resources for the Future – an environmental think tank with no particular partisan axe to grind – concluded that much of the effect was simply to subsidise purchases that would have taken place anyway.

I always thought that programme was a waste of money.

I agree, it does sound daft to try to stimulate the economy by handing out money to people who were planning to buy cars anyway. But if they spent $4000 less on their car than they would otherwise have done, perhaps they spent that money on something else.

Anyway, you're getting distracted by those sensible cost–benefit questions that Keynes warned us about. I'm not arguing that governments never back stupid projects. I'm arguing that if your economy's in a slump, then even stupid projects can give it a boost. It might have made perfect macro-economic sense for Obama to propose burying the clunkers and digging them up again.

All right, I can see why it's hard to be confident about the size of the multiplier. But still, there must be some estimates out there.

There are. For instance, the International Monetary Fund spent much of the financial crisis arguing that spending multipliers were around 0.5. Then, in late 2012, they announced they'd got it wrong and the multiplier was at least 0.7 and perhaps as high as 1.7.

That sounds like a pretty big error. How could they have got it so wrong?

Because they were looking at historical experience. Most recessions are not deep and prolonged slumps, and so in most cases when government ramps up spending, the economy will push back, as we discussed: prices will tend to rise and so will interest rates. But the recession of 2008 was no ordinary recession – the extreme assumptions we've been making, of weak demand, slack capacity and rock-bottom interest rates, have been all too realistic in the crisis.

The IMF's admission caused such a fuss because many countries had been responding to the recession not by increasing government spending, but by cutting it. It's a debate that has polarised politics in many countries since the crisis began – should the government be borrowing to try to boost the economy, or tightening its belt in a time of crisis? As political leaders and moods have changed since the financial crisis began, stimulus packages and austerity measures

have been introduced, denounced, withdrawn and reintro-
duced. The thing is that, just as borrowing to stimulate the
economy is much more effective when the multiplier is 1.7
than 0.5, likewise cutting spending when the multiplier is
1.7 is far more damaging than cutting when the multiplier
is 0.5. If you have a multiplier of 0.5, a spending cut of a
pound shrinks the economy as a whole by fifty pence; the
government spends a pound less, while the private sector
grows by fifty pence to fill some of that slack. But with a
multiplier of 1.7, when government spending shrinks, the
private sector shrinks too.

The IMF was admitting that it hadn't realised how much
damage government spending cuts would do to economic
growth. The reason the Fund felt it had got it wrong is quite
simple: the relatively mild recessions it had been analysing
were a poor guide to the much more serious recessions seen
around the developed world since 2008. The IMF's historical
evidence simply wasn't terribly relevant.

**And the IMF are supposed to be world-leading experts, I
assume? It's not very reassuring that they can get things so
wrong.**

Indeed not, and their error was pretty elementary. At least it
wasn't as basic as the mistake that embarrassed two Harvard
professors when they weighed into the debate about spending
cuts.

Which was?

Carmen Reinhart and Ken Rogoff presented a research paper called *Growth in a Time of Debt* in 2010, at a time when politicians everywhere were fiercely arguing about the wisdom of getting into further debt in the hopes of kickstarting the economy. From a bunch of statistical correlations between countries' growth rates and their debt/GDP ratios – which are a simple way to measure how much money a country's government has borrowed, relative to how big the economy is – Reinhart and Rogoff presented what quickly became a famous result: if a country's debt/GDP ratio rises above 90 per cent, economic growth tends to be substantially slower.

Politicians who favoured spending cuts jumped on this result, as you might expect. Paul Ryan, later the vice-presidential running mate of Mitt Romney, mentioned the 90 per cent growth collapse while arguing the case for the budget proposals that made his name. Olli Rehn, the European Union's top man on economics, also mentioned the 90 per cent cutoff. Professors Reinhart and Rogoff were invited to address a group of US senators. And their work was much mentioned by journalists. It was seen as relevant, of course, because efforts to simulate the economy involved cutting taxes, increasing government spending, and borrowing more money in the short term – which for many countries meant approaching or exceeding that dangerous-sounding 90 per cent debt/GDP ratio.

Now the story switches to the University of Massachusetts, Amherst, where a graduate student in economics, Thomas Herndon, was set a routine assignment: choose an interesting economics paper, get the data, and try to repeat the analysis.

This is called a replication exercise and it's good practice for young researchers. Herndon picked the Reinhart-Rogoff research, and quickly ran into trouble: he simply could not replicate the results from *Growth in a Time of Debt*. And of course his heart sank because, well, he was just a student and Reinhart and Rogoff were Harvard professors.

Eventually, Thomas Herndon approached Reinhart and Rogoff directly, and they sent him not only the data that was publicly available from their website, but the actual spreadsheet they had used to crunch the numbers. And he found – after blinking, rubbing his eyes and asking his girlfriend to check – that Carmen Reinhart and Ken Rogoff had made a pretty basic error in Excel: they missed out some of the rows, and thus didn't include the data for Australia, Austria, Belgium, Canada and Denmark.

Oops.

Oops. Actually, Herndon raised other question marks about the paper that ended up making a much bigger difference. He found that when more recently available data was included, the results changed substantially. He also picked a methodological fight with Reinhart and Rogoff; who wins that one is more a matter of opinion. Of course, pro-stimulus politicians and commentators milked the discovery of errors with the paper just as enthusiastically as pro-austerity politicians had milked the original paper.

This was overblown on both sides. An Excel spreadsheet full of correlations from wildly different countries in wildly different circumstances didn't prove much in the first place, so discovering errors in that spreadsheet doesn't disprove much, either. The bottom line is that lots of debt seems to be correlated with lower growth, as you would expect, but that eye-catchingly sharp cut-off at 90 per cent is imaginary. And finding a correlation is no proof that debt causes slow growth: the idea that slow growth causes debt is at least as plausible.[2]

This scepticism about data is a bit depressing.

Data and evidence are important, but in macroeconomics we just don't have enough data to be conclusive – so for now the data will only be part of any argument.

Think of it this way. If you really wanted to run a rigorous economic experiment, you'd take every economy in the world, and you'd split them into two groups at random. One group of economies would get a big fiscal stimulus. The other group would get nothing. You'd see what happened to growth rates in each group. That's as close as you could get to a nice clean macroeconomic experiment, and even then there would be some confusion in the data, because the no-stimulus countries would be trading with countries that had received the stimulus. If you really want to run this kind of experiment, just apply to the United Nations and let me know how you get on. Until then, let's simply acknowledge that the way macroeconomic policy is actually conducted is as far as possible from a robust scientific experiment, and I doubt that's going to change in a hurry.

There are some general things we can say about the likely

relative size of multipliers in different kinds of economy. A study by Ethan Ilzetzki, Enrique G. Mendoza and Carlos A. Vegh[3] – which concluded that multipliers are larger in economies that don't trade internationally much – doesn't just refer to North Korea, but also to the United States, because the US economy is so large that the domestic market looms large relative to exports and imports. That makes sense – if you have a large domestic market it's less likely that your stimulus will end up in the coffers of French vineyards. (An aside here: if you add up US exports and imports, the total will be around 20–25 per cent of GDP. That figure is around 50 per cent for many European economies, 100 per cent for South Korea, over 150 per cent for Estonia, and over 300 per cent for Singapore and Hong Kong. Recently economists have been arguing over whether Estonia's austerity was a success story or not; an interesting question in its own right, but one that tells us nothing at all about whether the US should be engaged in stimulus or austerity.)[4]

Ilzetzki and co. also concluded that multipliers are larger in economies with fixed exchange rates, such as ones that belong to the Eurozone. This also makes sense – we already know that sticky prices are a key explanation for why an economy gets stuck in a recession, and a fixed exchange rate is a very important, very sticky price. Painstaking as this research is, though, it deserves – like the IMF's – to be filed under 'best guess' rather than 'cast-iron proof'.

But I need practical advice. I understand that the facts are murky – just give me your best shot.

OK. Here's my four-step guide to effective fiscal policy in a crisis.

Step one: Start thinking about this when you're not in a crisis. Prepare the ground. If you're going to want to borrow money in a recession, you're going to need people to be willing to lend you that money, so it really helps if you begin the recession without being hugely in debt already. Unfortunately, very few governments take this advice. (I should admit that there are exceptions. Ireland and Spain both had low and falling debt before the crisis, but the recession was so deep and their banks so vulnerable that both countries struggled to find people willing to lend to them. The United States and Japan looked much more profligate, with persistent deficits and higher debt. But neither country has any trouble finding willing lenders. Life can be unfair.)

Another thing you should do when times are good is identify some big public investment projects with reasonable benefits, conduct all your due diligence, and then keep them on the shelf. That way, you're not going to waste precious time in a recession dithering about whether to build airports or hire street sweepers or bury chocolate coins. All you have to do is take a plan off the shelf, dust it off and put it into action. There are always big infrastructure projects worth doing sooner or later; best to actually do them when the economy is depressed. If you've misdiagnosed the situation and your infrastructure fails to provide any stimulus to the slumped economy as a whole, you still have the benefits of having a new road, hospital or power station.

Step two: When the crisis hits, use monetary policy as your first line of defence. Cutting interest rates is simple, relatively quick, and easy to reverse if the economy recovers and inflation begins to rise. Monetary policy is better understood than fiscal stimulus, and more likely to have been placed under the supervision of technocrats – independent central bankers – who are less influenced by the rough and tumble of short-term political expediency. It's also likely to be enough to stimulate the economy out of a recession that's short and shallow.

There will always be people who, for ideological reasons, like the idea of the government spending more money, and they'll be first in line to explain that fiscal stimulus is a nobrainer. Usually they will be wrong. They'll be wrong if the recession is a mild one, if monetary policy has plenty of scope (i.e., if interest rates are well above zero), and if the economy is small and open with a flexible exchange rate. They'll probably be wrong if even some subset of those conditions applies.

It just so happens that in the most recent crisis, interest rates *were* near zero; the economies involved *were* large and often had fixed exchange rates; the recession was *not* mild. There is every reason to believe that fiscal stimulus was entirely appropriate. But these are lessons applying to an important and recent case. They are not universal truths.

Conversely, there will always be people who, for ideological reasons, hate the idea of government spending and will be first in line to explain that stimulus spending is wasteful and simply gets in the way of more efficient private projects. They are often right about that, but recently – at least according to my reading of the evidence – they've been wrong.

Step three: If the recession is starting to look long and deep, go to the shelf for those projects you identified earlier and start building, quickly. A problem with many stimulus spending schemes is that they take so long to get started that the recession is over before the foundations are laid. If you spend money on less-than-brilliant projects in an economy that has already recovered, all you'll do is fuel inflation while making the economy as a whole work less effectively.

Step four: Make sure your fiscal stimulus projects don't make people nervous about how you're ever going to repay your debts. If that happens, investors will become unwilling to lend you the money you need to borrow, and taxpayers will start to think about saving for future tax hikes.

On the taxation side, you could announce a temporary cut in sales tax or VAT. This encourages people to spend money now because they know it will buy less in future, and makes clear that the money is going to be recouped later. On the spending side, aim for investment projects that are one-off by their nature – build a new high-speed railway line, fix potholes in the roads, that kind of thing. Unlike burying and exhuming chocolate coins, these kinds of projects will be helpful after the recession is over, and minimise the risk of creating vested interests.

That advice might seem blindingly obvious, but, again, unfortunately many governments don't take it – they tend to cut investment during recessions because it is politically much easier to do that than to cut pensions, civil service salaries and welfare benefits.

So, let's recap – we've covered monetary policy and fiscal policy, and I understand what to do when my economy hits trouble. Good. This is looking easier than I thought.

Then it's time for me to throw a spanner in the works by explaining that pretty much everything I've told you so far has come from one school of macroeconomic thought – the Keynesians. There's another group of economists who think Keynes got it all wrong. They're called classical economists, and we'd better take a look at what they have to say.

6

The prison-camp recession

'By April, 1945, chaos had replaced order in the economic sphere: sales were difficult, prices lacked stability. Economics has been defined as the science of distributing limited means among unlimited and competing ends. On 12th April, with the arrival of elements of the 30th US Infantry Division, the ushering in of an age of plenty demonstrated the hypothesis that with infinite means economic organisation and activity would be redundant, as every want could be satisfied without effort.'

R.A. Radford

Right, then: tell me about classical economists. Where do they differ from Keynesians?

Remember Keynes's 'magneto trouble' line, and fourteen-year-old Bill Phillips poking around under the bonnet of the broken-down old truck? Well, there's a long tradition of 'classical' economists who have refused to accept the metaphor. Classical economists treat economies as well-oiled machines. In this tradition, recessions are not economic malfunctions; economies don't break down, like an old truck can. Instead, they are the result of either incompetent policy or something called exogenous shocks.

Exogenous shocks? What on earth are they?

They're things, good or bad, that strike your economy from outside. To extend the metaphor, classical economists believe that if your truck has a problem it's nothing to do with the engine. Either you're driving it badly or you've been side-swiped by a passing bus. Poking around under the bonnet with a spanner is only going to make things worse.

Are they right?

Let's just say that their perspective is well worth considering. The best way for us to get to grips with the classical point of view is to look at another recession. In the same way that we looked at the Keynesian view through the recession in the Washington DC babysitting co-op, we can get our heads around the classical view by telling the story of a recession in a German prisoner-of-war camp during the Second World War.

Come again? Did POW camps even have economies, let alone recessions?

They did indeed, and we know this thanks to Robert A. Radford. Radford studied economics at Cambridge University, and worked at the International Monetary Fund. In between, he spent half the war in a German prison camp, and on his release wrote an article in *Economica*, the flagship journal of the London School of Economics. Radford saw his article, 'The Economic Organisation of a POW Camp', primarily as a piece of sociology, analysing the unexpected way in which economic institutions arose in very strange and difficult circumstances.[1] But we are interested in how it can illustrate the classical view of economic recessions.

The building blocks of the POW camp economy were parcels of food and cigarettes that the prisoners received from the Red Cross. These parcels were standardised – everybody got the same, beyond the occasional package from home. Occasionally the Red Cross received bumper supplies, or ran short; in those circumstances everybody enjoyed a surplus or a shortage. Naturally enough, while prisoners had equal rations, they did not have identical preferences. The Sikhs didn't have much use for their rations of beef or razor blades, for example; the French were desperate for more coffee; the English wanted more tea.

There was not much production in the prison-camp economy, but there was some: some men would, for instance, offer to polish boots or press uniforms. One entrepreneurial fellow set up a cart selling tea, coffee and cocoa. At one stage he enjoyed the services of a chartered accountant, as well as paying other prisoners to gather fuel. And there was government provision too, of a sort: the senior British officer set up a camp shop and restaurant, including live entertainment. Chiefly, though, the POW-camp economy was built on trading, and plenty of trading took place.

Market institutions emerged spontaneously. There was a currency: the cigarette, which was portable and reasonably homogeneous. Non-smokers, not being tempted to burn their 'money', were naturally at a distinct advantage. (The cigarette wasn't a perfect currency: cigarettes could be 'sweated' by rolling them back and forth between the fingers to shake a little tobacco out. The well-filled cigarettes would then be kept while the skinnier ones were used as cash – an illustration of a well-known economic principle called 'Gresham's Law'.)

There was a futures market: with bread rations handed out on Monday, on Sunday evening 'bread now' traded at a premium to 'bread Monday'. There were even imports and exports – coffee would go 'over the wire' to be sold in black-market cafés in Munich.

You mean the prison camp exported products to civilian Germany?

Amazingly, yes. At times, the Red Cross was able to supply the prisoners with things that German civilians themselves couldn't get. And of course, when there is an opportunity to supply a scarce resource, the profit motive will usually find a way. Middlemen prospered, especially if they had the ability to speak multiple languages or friendly relations with German guards to let them visit different parts of the camp.

Presumably this was a trader's paradise?

Less than you might think. There were stories, says Radford, 'of a padre who started off round the camp with a tin of cheese and five cigarettes and returned to his bed with a complete parcel in addition to his original cheese and cigarettes; the market was not yet perfect'. But these were tales (and probably exaggerated ones) of life in the chaotic transit camps. Once Radford arrived at a permanent camp, he found that prices tended to be stable and well known, precisely because there were middlemen around, seeking out bargains and arbitrage opportunities.

But while prices didn't bounce around like the offers to naive tourists at a bazaar, they did move in response to broader developments – for example, an influx of new, hungry prisoners of war would generally drive up the price of food; when the weather was hot, the price of cocoa fell and the price of soap rose; dried fruit prices rose sharply and stayed high after someone discovered that, in Radford's words, 'raisins and sugar could be turned into an alcoholic liquor of remarkable potency'.

These are all examples of what economists call an 'exogenous' shock – meaning that it isn't produced inside the economic system under consideration.

Hold on – the raisin liquor was invented inside the economic system, wasn't it? Or are you saying the recipe arrived in the form of a telegram from a distillery in Belgium?

No, and this is where the word 'exogenous' gets a little slippery. The point is that it wasn't a part of the economic system that we might model with our usual equations of supply and demand. To take a more modern example, the development of the mobile phone was an event that took place inside the economy – but an economist would treat it as an 'exogenous technology shock' because most economic models usually don't even try to incorporate such things.

Now, towards the end of the war, the camp economy suffered its biggest exogenous shock of all – the supply of Red Cross parcels gradually dried up. This caused a recession – volumes of trade became smaller and smaller. But unlike the recession in the babysitting co-op, sticky prices had nothing to do with it. There was, in fact, an inexorable rise in the price of cigarettes, which were being smoked at a much faster rate than the Red Cross parcels could replenish them. In difficult circumstances, the well-oiled economic machine worked just as it should.

Why didn't prices stick?

It's a fascinating question, as Radford certainly noted the same psychological tendencies that ordinarily can lead to sticky prices. There were constant efforts, both on the part of the senior officers imprisoned in the camp, and in the form of pure social pressure, to stop the prices moving too far from what was regarded as reasonable – the 'just price'. Radford pointed out that the just price was a mysterious thing: 'Everyone knew what it was, though no one could explain why it should be so.' Those whose trades varied too much from the just price faced official censure from the senior British officer, and they also faced contempt from ordinary prisoners – feelings of anger that we've seen quantified by the research of Daniel Kahneman.

But despite the outrage at unjust prices, trades at such prices continued. I suspect the reason is that in a comfortable Capitol Hill social set, social pressure is more important than the convenience of actually trading some babysitting. In the desperation of a prison camp, however, social pressure was less powerful than the desire to get hold of bread, or cigarettes, at whatever price the market would bear. Whatever the reason, says Radford, 'prices moved with the supply of cigarettes, and refused to stay fixed in accordance with a theory of ethics'.

I realise that it sounds odd to contrast a prison camp with a babysitting co-op, but I think it can shed a lot of light on contemporary arguments that economists have – for instance, over the question of stimulus versus austerity.

Let me see if I've got the difference. The recession in the babysitting co-op was because people were held back from making trades they wanted to make. The recession in the prison camp was simply because there was less stuff available to trade.

That's pretty much it. To recast the difference in economic terms, the babysitting recession was a failure of demand, caused by the design of the co-op babysitting economy. The prison-camp recession was a failure of supply, and that failure was nothing to do with the economy of the prison camp itself and everything to do with the exogenous shock of fewer Red Cross parcels.

The modern economy doesn't depend on Red Cross parcels, though. Give me some recent, real-world examples of exogenous shocks.

I've already mentioned one – the invention of the mobile phone, which reminds us that these shocks can be good news as well as bad. Another is the dramatic growth of China, which has had a huge effect on other national economies – for example, making imported manufactured goods cheaper, and driving down interest rates on government bonds. Another was the Tōhoku earthquake and tsunami, which as well as killing almost twenty thousand people destroyed a lot of productive infrastructure in Japan, most notoriously the Fukushima Daiichi nuclear power plant.

But the most important exogenous shock was probably what happened to the price of crude oil in the 1970s – in fact, the events even became known as the 'oil shock'. The first wave happened in late 1973. Egypt and Syria had launched a surprise attack against Israel, and Israel's counter-attack had been backed by the United States. Against this backdrop, Arab members of OPEC, the Organisation of Petroleum Exporting Countries, announced an embargo on oil exports. The price of oil quickly doubled, reaching its highest for almost a century after decades of slow and remarkably stable decline in real terms. The effect was extremely damaging to Western economies, which used gas-guzzling cars and generated much of their electricity from oil-fired power stations. The second leg of the crisis began in 1979 after disruption to Iranian oil supplies during the revolution, followed by the Iran–Iraq War, which began in 1980. The price of oil doubled again, to levels not seen since the 1860s, when oil had been irrelevant to the global energy mix.

The oil crisis dealt a heavy blow to Western economies, which suffered multiple recessions in the 1970s, 'stagflation' – the combination of stagnant economic growth with inflation – and finally a deep double recession in the United States and the United Kingdom in the early 1980s, as the monetary authorities clamped down on inflation to the exclusion of all other goals.

But the crisis also dealt a heavy blow to Keynesianism, the dominant school of macroeconomics of the day. Even influential free-market critics such as Milton Friedman were operating in the Keynesian paradigm in the 1960s, using Keynesian analysis to understand slumps, even if Friedman reached different policy conclusions.[2] The oil shock was a shock to professional economists as much as to the economy itself. The traditional Keynesian remedy, which was to print money to stimulate demand, was entirely counter-productive in the face of a shock to supply. Inflation increased but demand did not. It is hardly surprising that the entire episode sparked fresh interest in the classical view of the economy as a machine that worked well but could be derailed by external shocks.

Bear in mind that there was a miniature oil shock in 1990 after Saddam Hussein invaded Kuwait: prices again doubled, although the price shock lasted only a few months rather than several years. Is it a coincidence that countries ranging from the United States and France to the United Kingdom and Japan all promptly suffered a recession? Even the US recession of 2001 and the global financial crisis of 2007–2008 were both preceded by substantial oil price shocks. Most economists don't think the oil shocks were decisive in these two recent cases, but there is a thoughtful and well-informed minority who believe these oil price shocks formed a very significant part of the overall crisis.

So the idea of exogenous shocks is now here to stay. Such shocks affect supply rather than demand. They change the productive potential of the economy – either negatively or positively – and the economy will adjust in all sorts of ways. This may involve years of fluctuations, just as a jelly will wobble backwards and forwards several times after a single shove. Classical economists say we should resist the urge of a Bill Phillips to get under the bonnet and try to fix the economy, which was so counter-productive in the 1970s. We should just step back and let the economy get on with adjusting on its own.

That would make my job of running the economy a lot easier, I suppose. But should I listen to the classical economists?

The babysitting co-op should be all the proof you need that you shouldn't always listen to them. The co-op recession was nothing to do with the productive potential of the co-op itself: that productive potential was ready to be tapped throughout. The fact that it was not tapped was nothing to do with exogenous forces. It was a failure of the economic machine, and it had the potential to be fixed with some deft economic tinkering.

The question we have to answer is whether more recessions are like babysitting co-op recessions or POW-camp recessions. When we try to understand the economy, should we start with the assumption that it functions smoothly, like the prison camp, but is buffeted by external shocks and hamstrung by policy errors? Or should our starting point be that the economy itself is, like the babysitting co-op, prone to malfunction – and needs Bill Phillips-style tinkerers to keep it ticking over nicely?

Another way to frame that dilemma is to ask what limits economic output, supply or demand? The French classical economist Jean-Baptiste Say coined 'Say's Law', which simply says that 'supply creates its own demand'. In the prison-camp context this means: 'don't worry about the pricing system, worry about whether the Red Cross parcels have arrived.'

But in a real economy surely supply *doesn't* create its own demand?

It does if prices adjust smoothly enough. Producers will do their thing, making goods and offering services, and at the right price they'll be able to sell these goods and services. If the price of goods and services collapses, so does the income of producers – but then, the prices of the goods and services they will buy with their income will have also fallen. As prices and incomes are all falling, in real terms nobody is any worse off.

Say's Law tells us that it is simply impossible for an economy to suffer a general glut in demand. Instead, prices will adjust until supply equals demand. And if you believe this, then the only way that an economy can suffer a recession is if there's a problem with supply, as there was in the POW camp.

The prison-camp experience is very much in line with the classical view of recessions: prices did adjust, markets did clear, but because of an exogenous shock, life was harsh, and if policy did anything at all it made things worse.

Hadn't Say heard of the babysitting recession?

No, he died in 1832. The Sweeneys published their article 145 years too late for him to benefit from the case study.

The babysitting recession is an example of 'Keynes's Law' – 'lack of demand creates its own lack of supply'. In a Keynesian recession, Say's Law doesn't hold, and it is possible for supply to stand idle for lack of demand. If consumers don't want to spend, instead preferring to save or pay off their debts, perhaps no price cut will tempt them to change their mind – or perhaps a price cut would, but the price cut does not come because prices are sticky. Business investment might take up the slack but then again it might not, because why would businesses invest when they already have factories and shops standing quiet, dark and empty?

In this Keynesian view, a recession develops simply because there are too many would-be sellers but not enough buyers – and the babysitting co-op is the perfect illustration of this occurring. Plenty of people were happy to act as babysitters, so supply was not a problem. But too few people actually wanted to use the babysitters because of the shortage of scrip. The babysitting co-op suffered a recession purely because of a lack of demand.

So we've found an example when Say's Law applies, and another when Keynes's Law does. It sounds like neither of them is really a law at all.

Yup. This is social science – what did you expect? Sometimes an economy's output is constrained by the demand for goods and services (Keynes's Law) and sometimes it is constrained by their potential supply (Say's Law).

This isn't helping. Is there a way to reconcile the classical and Keynesian views?

As it happens, there is. In fact, for many economists there's no need to reconcile anything. Sometimes economies suffer from demand shocks and sometimes they suffer from supply shocks. Both the Keynesian and classical perspectives can be helpful, depending on the circumstances. There's a reconciliation on a geekier level, too. Much of modern macroeconomics is some kind of synthesis between classical and Keynesian analytical techniques – but that is far too technical for us to worry about.

But there is also a really simple way to combine the two views. We need to introduce a concept you'll hear discussed often in economics – the 'short run' and the 'long run'.

Most economists would agree that in the short run, it is Keynes's Law that is relevant. Many recessions happen because of a lack of demand, and this lack of demand can be fixed by smart policymakers working with the right tools. And most economists would also agree that in the long run, it is Say's Law that counts: ultimately the output of an economy is determined by its capacity to supply goods and services. Given enough time, demand will catch up and that potential to supply will be fulfilled.

Even this is an oversimplification. The 1970s oil shocks happened very quickly, but they were a classical problem and Keynesian, demand-side approaches would not have helped. Still, 'short-run Keynes, long-run classical' is not a bad rule of thumb.

So now I need to know: how long is the short run, exactly? Didn't Keynes say, 'in the long run we're all dead'?

He did indeed – and that's an interesting meditation on the human condition, but not terribly satisfying as a piece of economics. But the point is it's not enough to say that in the long run everything will be fine, because the short run can be pretty long. More recently, Paul Krugman has been arguing that, in the real economy as with the babysitting co-op, the short run can last for many years unless policy action is taken.

Others disagree, arguing that if an economy is suffering long-term ill-effects, that doesn't reflect a stretched-out demand problem, but damage to the supply potential of the economy. The UK's Office for Budget Responsibility (OBR) – a body set up to cast an independent eye over the government's spending projections – has taken the view that the banking crisis did permanent damage to the UK's economic capacity, for example by driving fundamentally healthy companies into bankruptcy. If the OBR is right then Professor Krugman's remedy – that the government should spend money to prop up demand – risks cramming spending power into an economy unable to deliver. The result will be inflation, or a rise in imports, or both.

You're telling me that the concepts of short run and long run are so slippery, experts can't agree which one we're in.

I'm afraid so. There is a lot of disagreement. Some of this is very technical – what exactly the best modelling strategy is, which simplifications are reasonable and which are not. But the real disagreement is diagnosing what the problem is: is it lack of demand, or lack of supply?

This matters, as the different situations call for very different solutions on the part of the authorities.

Meaning me.

Meaning you. If you think we are currently suffering a Keynesian recession then your remedy is pretty simple: first, use monetary policy by cutting interest rates and perhaps printing money; if you are concerned that that might not be enough, cut taxes or increase spending, as described in the previous chapter.

If, on the other hand, the basic problem is supply then we are in a classical recession and your answer is different: cut spending and raise taxes, because the economy's potential has shrunk and you'd better adjust to the painful new reality. And start thinking about whether there is anything you can do to expand the long-run supply potential of the economy.

So the stakes are quite high, here. This may explain why the disagreement is occasionally impolite.

I can see that. So how do I diagnose whether an economy is suffering from short-run lack of demand, or long-run lack of supply? I'm imagining it can't be that easy, or economists wouldn't spend so much energy trying to scratch each other's eyes out.

You're right, of course. This isn't easy. Time for a new chapter, I think.

7

Output gaps

**You were going to tell me how to tell the difference between
a prison-camp recession and a babysitting co-op recession.**

Yes. Economists talk about the 'output gap' – the gap between
actual economic output and potential output. The basic idea is
that if we were in a Keynesian, babysitting co-op recession then
there would be spare capacity that, with the right stimulus, we
could draw on. There would be an output gap, a gap between
actual output and what could potentially be produced.

'What could potentially be produced' sounds like another slippery concept.

I'm afraid it is. Potentially under what circumstances? If the central bank printed more money? If employers were more confident? If workers were able to psychically identify job vacancies and teleport to them? If wishes were horses?

The uncomfortable truth is that 'potential output' is a notional number. You're always going to be guessing. And inevitably, people's preconceptions are likely to have considerable bearing on what they guess. Economists who find Keynesian models convincing and expect to see Keynesian recessions will tend to believe that they see slack in the economy. Economists with a more classical approach start from the point that, by definition, actual output and potential output are the same thing: economies don't malfunction and so if there's some kind of slowdown, by definition it must be a decrease in the economy's potential.

But it's not just a matter of guesswork plus ideology. There are four main indicators that we can look at to give us a sense of whether the output gap is small – suggesting a supply-driven recession – or large, meaning that deficient demand is the problem and some kind of stimulus is called for.

First: the trend. Modern economies tend to have a typical growth rate. This is a function of demography (children grow up and start finding jobs) and of new technologies and improved working practices being developed and gradually adopted. If growth suddenly drops below that trend, that suggests an output gap is opening up. The gap will stay open until there's a growth spurt that makes up for all the lost time.

For example, let's say that your economy usually grows at

3 per cent a year. There's a brief recession, meaning the economy shrinks for a few months, and over the course of the year, growth is zero. At the end of that year, a first guess at the output gap would be 3 per cent, which represents the growth that should have happened, but didn't. Let's say that the year after, the economy is still a bit weak, and grows at 2 per cent – a percentage point below trend. Now the output gap is 4 per cent, reflecting the continuing failure of actual production to keep pace with population growth and what we might reasonably expect from the march of new technology. But never fear; for the following two years, growth is 5 per cent a year. The output gap closes, the economy has made up for lost time, and all is now well. Any stimulus of the economy – tax cuts, spending gimmicks, low interest rates – should be removed, because from now on it cannot sustainably aid any recovery, but will merely lead to inflation.

But hang on – if you assume that output follows a smooth trend then you are basically assuming that all recessions are Keynesian recessions. Aren't you?

Very perceptive. The smooth trend approach assumes that an economy's potential follows this serene, imperturbable course, and that any divergence from this requires stimulus to get back on track. The whole point of the classical view of recessions is that potential output is just as uneven as actual output – the trend, on this view, is not a hugely helpful guide.

However, it's clear from the recent crisis that there are limits to the usefulness of this classical view. Falls below trend were simply astonishing. In the UK, for instance, trend growth was just over 2.5 per cent a year, but in late 2008 the economy contracted sharply. By the end of 2012, the economy was almost 15 per cent below trend, and growth well below 2.5 per cent a year suggests an ever-widening output gap.

A hard-line classical economist would simply say: tough. Output collapsed by almost 15 per cent below trend; therefore potential output also collapsed by the same amount. But most people would look at the numbers and conclude that it simply isn't plausible for potential output to fall so far in such a short space of time – for so many factories and offices suddenly to find themselves not just unused but unusable. A smaller fall, and particularly a more gradual fall behind the old trend, might well suggest that the trend itself has changed. But 15 per cent in just a handful of years seems vast. If the recession is really big, then surely some part of it must be a problem with demand, and some kind of stimulus could help output to recover quickly, at least part of the way.

The second thing we could look at when considering whether there really is an output gap or not is unemployment. If you suddenly have lots of unemployed people, surely that's a good indicator of slack in the economic system. It's a strong indicator that stimulus is required.

Now, again, a determinedly classical view of the world would say: not so fast. There are unemployed workers. But at least for now, they are also unemployable. A shock has hit the economy, and the old skills are not valued any more. Workers will need time and perhaps help to retrain, to move to a different area, and to find their feet in a totally new industry. Cutting interest rates won't really help, and neither will cutting taxes: this is a matter of patience, not of stimulus.

Workers cannot change careers overnight. Directly employing these workers to bury and disinter chocolate coins will be unsustainable: it will remove them from the unemployment statistics for a while but will simply postpone a painful adjustment. All these attempts at stimulus will prove misplaced. They will merely create inflation – just as we saw in the 1970s, with high levels of inflation and yet sluggish growth and lots of people looking for work.

There must be ways to tell if the unemployed really are unemployable.

As it happens, there are. A tell-tale sign of this classical structural misalignment would be that some sectors boom, with full employment and rising wages, as they try desperately to recruit qualified workers; other sectors stagnate. But in the US, unemployment rates rose sharply in most sectors of the economy following the onset of the crisis in 2007. They also rose for most kinds of worker. Paul Krugman, an evangelist for the Keynesian view, argues that this is good evidence for a general problem with demand, not an economy knocked sideways by a structural shock.[1]

In the UK, the picture is more puzzling. Unemployment rose, of course, but by much less than one would have expected given the severity of the recession. The logical implication of this is that productivity per worker fell. The effect was very large – if I were to draw you a graph of the relationship between economic output and employment growth for the last forty years or so, you would be astonished at how closely they usually stick to each other, and how far apart they drifted during the recession. Now, part of that will be part-time work becoming more common. And part will be 'labour hoarding' – firms have fewer customers but they have good workers that they don't want to lose, going through all the expense of compensating them and then the expense of re-hiring unskilled workers later. But that can't be the whole story, because employers started hiring briskly once weak growth resumed. If labour hoarding was the answer, you'd expect hiring to dry up temporarily, because employers already had plenty of underemployed workers.

It all suggests that workers in the UK are simply producing less than they used to, which implies structural problems – in contrast to the US, a big classical element to the recession. What seems to be happening in the UK is a shift from higher-productivity industries, which are being forced to shrink, to lower-productivity industries which are growing. That's a textbook structural shift – metaphorically, there are fewer food parcels arriving. And maybe it shouldn't be such a shock that the UK has suffered structural damage. The country was heavily dependent on financial services, and financial services have never been quite the same since the banking crisis.

You promised four ways to try to tell if there's an output gap. What are the other two?

You could send a questionnaire round to companies and ask them whether they have spare capacity. In the UK, the answer was clear: despite this large gap between actual output and trend output, companies said that they didn't have much spare capacity. That in itself suggests structural problems and a classical, prison-camp recession. It suggests that monetary and fiscal stimulus won't help much. Still, you never know. Perhaps firms are at 'full capacity' in the sense that their existing workers are all flat-out, but they could easily hire more and expand quite quickly if, say, they had more customers or access to a reasonably priced loan from a bank.

And a final clue to whether you have a Keynesian recession or a classical recession is inflation. If inflation drops to a low level for an extended period of time that suggests weak demand. If inflation is buoyant despite slow growth, that suggests that the cause lies on the supply side. Even here, there's no guarantee – inflation will also be affected by other factors, such as the price of oil.

None of these four clues seems especially conclusive.

You didn't expect this to be easy, did you? If economic policy was something we understood as well as we understand – say – building a bridge, there wouldn't be such arguments about it.

The fact is, there's a fundamental problem that holds us back when we're trying to tell whether a recession is being caused by a lack of demand – that is, a babysitting co-op recession – or a lack of supply, like in the prison camp: you can't really observe one of demand or supply without the other. One of the great classical economists, Alfred Marshall, once said that trying to figure out whether supply or demand is doing the work is like trying to figure out which blade of the scissors cuts the paper.

And actually, it's even trickier than that – because unlike with scissor blades, the boundary between demand and supply is itself somewhat blurred. If an economy contracts because of a problem with demand, the damage may eventually bleed over into supply. In the case of the babysitting co-op, for example, we might imagine couples getting so frustrated at the difficulty of getting a sitter that they resign from the co-op and install home cinema. Then they are no longer available to babysit for others: a recession that initially had nothing to do with the supply potential of the economy eventually damages that supply potential.

In a more complex economy, skilled workers might emigrate; companies going out of business might lead to the loss of institutional knowledge that cannot easily be replaced by new startups; machinery might rust; factories and office buildings might fall into disrepair; workers might spend so long on the dole that they lose their work ethic, or their skills, or perhaps just the confidence of employers who should be willing to give them a chance, but aren't. For all these reasons, a short-run demand-led recession may turn into long-run supply-side damage.

When a business goes bankrupt, for instance, there will be disruption. Workers will be unemployed; a shop, factory or office will be empty; the bankrupt company's suppliers will have slack capacity and will need to find a new customer to fill their order books. In principle the workers, the empty premises, the slack capacity are all supply potential that can instantly be redeployed to a new purpose. In reality it will take time and it may also take a big investment of resources: the workers may need to go back to college, the business premises bulldozed and replaced. Lack of demand in the short run has produced a dearth of supply in the medium to long run.

Hang on, though. If demand bleeds into supply is there really such a dilemma after all? Why not treat every recession with a Keynesian remedy in the short run while looking at classical supply-side problems in the long run?

There's a lot to be said for that idea. Economic pundits like to emphasise their disagreements, but there's often no contradiction between pursuing Keynesian stimulus – whether fiscal or monetary – and also looking at structural reform.

For a much-discussed version of this false dilemma, consider the *New York Times* columnist David Brooks, who in May 2012 wrote an opinion piece called 'The Structural Revolution'. Brooks divided the world into 'cyclicalists' and 'structuralists'. Cyclicalists are Brooks's version of Keynesians and structuralists is Brooks's term for classicals. Sort of. Except that Brooks then worries that his cyclicalists are missing 'the core issues', that they 'believe that the level of government spending is the main factor in determining how fast an economy grows', and are 'papering over' structural problems with more debt.

That does sound quite a lot like what you're saying.

Brooks's column is fascinating because it's so nearly right, and yet it's wrong. There is always a question mark, in any recession, as to how far it's a problem of aggregate demand (and thus amenable to stimulus) and how far it's a problem of supply (and thus cannot be solved with stimulus). But usually it's not a case of either/or. It's a case of short run and long run. In the short run, most recessions have a Keynesian element and should be addressed with stimulus. The stimulus will usually come from the central bank, by the way, rather than from extra government spending. And in the long run it's always worth thinking about structural issues to raise the capacity of the economy to produce.

Indeed, you could even do both with the same policy – for example, spending during a recession on well-chosen infrastructure projects such as railways, road repairs or faster broadband. You'd be putting people to work who would otherwise be unemployed in the short term, and improving the structural capacity of the economy in the long term.

There are some risks with trying to do both, admittedly. If you instead pay people to bury and exhume chocolate, you're not going to be expanding the economy's capacity to produce. And, as we have seen, fiscal stimulus may be hard to scale back in the good times, allowing debt to slowly build up to unwise levels. A lot of countries, including the United States and the UK, entered the great recession with a fair bit of debt and a baked-in commitment to borrow money just to keep government running in the good times. That's not an ideal position to be in – and to be fair, it is not what the Keynesian approach actually demands.

As for structural reforms, it might seem like there's never a bad time to increase the underlying capacity of the economy – and that may be true if we're talking about a wisely chosen infrastructure project. But think about another structural reform that's often proposed: changing the law to make it easier for employers to sack workers. There are good reasons to believe that would also make the economy function more smoothly in the long run – employers would be less nervous of hiring people, and could give younger, unproven workers a chance without much risk. But what happens in the short run if you do that in the middle of a recession? It would enable employers to sack more of their existing employees, immediately depress demand even further and prolong the recession. The upside of the reform, faster job growth, would not make itself felt until the recession was over.

It feels like what you're saying is that I should run my economy like a tough bastard right-winger during a boom, and like a bleeding-heart left-winger during a recession.

That's not such a bad idea. A boom is a great time to trim spending, pay off debt, and try to make markets function better by reducing unnecessary regulations. These are all right-wing hobby-horses. A recession, however, is a terrible time to do those things. It's better to keep spending, run up debt, and launch big infrastructure projects.

Unfortunately, it seems we tend to get the opposite: in booms, we feel like we can afford to elect left-wing governments to improve labour protection and launch big public-sector projects, often running up debt in the process; then when trouble hits, we elect a right-wing government to slash the deficit, scrap investment projects and make a bonfire of labour protection regulations, all of which simply make the recession worse.

As we saw back in Chapter 1, ultimately the reason we should care about recessions is their human cost. I think it's time to turn our attention to understanding unemployment – a subject which is something of a puzzle.

8

The invention of unemployment

'The average man won't really do a day's work unless he is
caught and cannot get out of it. There is plenty of work
to do if people would do it.'

Henry Ford, March 1931[1]

What's so puzzling about unemployment?

It's one of the most basic problems of economics. Yet if you
approach it using one of the most fundamental concepts of
economics – 'supply and demand' – you don't get terribly far.
In theory, if companies want more workers, they should raise
wages. If they want fewer workers, they should lower wages.
If unemployed people want to find work, they should accept
lower wages. And if they remain unemployed, it must be
because they've decided they'd rather put their feet up. If you
follow that logic through, recessions are just great big holi-
days – unemployed people have taken a look at the wages
companies are willing to pay, and decided they'd rather relax
and wait for wages to rise to an acceptable level, which they
will do in a recovery.

Some of the more firmly classical economists seem to accept this story. But it's hard to make a case for it. For one thing, we know that wages often don't fall during a recession: companies will sack some people and keep others on at the old wage rates. For another thing, many unemployed people are extremely unhappy. If you take psychological research into happiness and economic circumstances seriously, you conclude that money itself only has a modest impact on people's satisfaction with their lives, but having a job is a far more important consideration. It's hard to square that with the idea that unemployed people have simply resigned because they're not satisfied with the pay.

But if you really want evidence that there's something missing with the simple supply-and-demand story, let me tell you a story about Henry Ford – the man who invented unemployment.

Invented unemployment? Don't you mean factory production lines, or the Model T?

Those too – and OK, it's an exaggeration. But it has a kernel of truth. Here's the story. At the start of 1914, Henry Ford, the founder and majority owner of the Ford Motor Company, introduced a new minimum wage of five dollars a day – more than twice the previous wage – while reducing the day from nine hours to eight. The result? Thousands of men braved the Detroit winter to throng around the Ford factory every day, hoping to get a job. One day there was a riot, and the police used a fire hose to try to disperse the crowds. The drenched men, their outer clothes freezing almost instantly in temperatures well below zero, withdrew to dry out or to change. Then they came straight back again.

The new wage, it should be said, didn't apply to everyone. There was a six-month probationary period and workers would miss out if they didn't satisfy Ford's paternalistic team of sociologists that they were heading a hygienic and prudent household. It may not be a surprise to hear that women were excluded too, although Ford officials told the *New York Times* that any woman who was head of her household would be eligible for the five-dollar pay rate, which they called a 'profit share'. Nevertheless, the five-dollar wage was paid to the majority of Ford workers. It was an astonishing move.[2]

I'll say. He must have been really struggling to recruit enough good workers, right?

Actually, no. You're certainly right to think that that's what a straightforward supply-and-demand explanation would predict. Ford's wage rise would make sense if he was having trouble recruiting the right calibre of worker. One could imagine that competitors in the fast-expanding motor industry of Detroit were bidding up wages – in red-hot labour markets, wages can indeed increase sharply at times. But no. The Detroit labour market at the time wasn't red hot; there was a recession taking place. The number of people granted poor relief in the area had almost quadrupled in the two years prior to Henry Ford's five-dollar day.

So Ford wasn't being outbid by his competitors, and nor did

his competitors see any immediate need to try to outbid him: one sanguine rival told the *Detroit News* that 'The Ford plant can only give employment to so many men and after that the others will have to seek employment in other plants at the prevailing wage.' In other words, once Ford had hired everybody he wanted, competitors would still be able to hire the rest at the going market rate for auto workers, which was less than half of what Ford had begun to pay.

We can tell that Ford wasn't interested in encouraging a broader pool of applicants from the fact that he actively discouraged some workers from applying – not surprisingly, when he had so many applicants they were rioting at the factory gates. After workers from all over America flocked to Detroit in the hope of a job at the Ford plant, the company announced that it wouldn't hire workers from out of town. It also moved to shut down consultancy companies which sent in applications on behalf of workers in exchange for a fee.

And it wasn't as if Ford was looking only for workers with the right skills: after all, he had systematically been phasing highly skilled craftsmen out of his factory. Five years previously, two-thirds of Ford's employees had been skilled craftsmen and his factory was more like a collection of separate mechanics' workshops, with each one taking a motley assortment of imperfect parts, made outside Ford, and carefully machining them and assembling them to produce a real hand-crafted vehicle. But by the time he introduced the five-dollar day, Ford had swept away this bespoke artisanship and focused his entire factory on producing, in a highly automated manner, a single make of car: the Model T. The workforce increased more than thirtyfold, and output increased by a similar amount. Ford's new system of making cars required large numbers of semi-skilled men, performing repetitive tasks. He wanted docile robots who would do what they were told, over and over again. (One worker grumbled that the monotony was driving him insane: 'If I keep putting on Nut No. 86 for about 86 more days, I will be Nut No. 86 in the Pontiac bughouse.') The last thing the company wanted was highly skilled generalists of the pre-Model T days, people with experience and opinions, who might have been harder to find.

In short, none of this suggests a company struggling with recruitment. That wasn't the reason Ford started paying much more generous wages.

Hmm. Maybe Ford was trying to get a reputation as a philanthropist?

It's another plausible-sounding theory. He was a rich man, after all, and his five-dollar working day made him famous – Ford was frequently on the front page of the *New York Times* in the months following its introduction.

But there are several reasons to be suspicious of this explanation. While the five-dollar workday was announced in grandiose terms to the local press in Detroit, it wasn't trumpeted any further than that, and the national and international attention seems to have come as a surprise. And Ford's company was only a few years into its prime: if Ford really wanted to devote himself to philanthropy, this would have been like Bill Gates turning his gaze to global poverty in around 1985, before Microsoft had really established itself as the software powerhouse it would later become. Given that the five-dollar workday came so early in Ford's career, it would have been an extraordinarily large philanthropic giveaway: the pay increase was around half the company's expected profits. And Henry Ford didn't own Ford outright; he was merely the majority shareholder. Had he really decided to funnel half the company's cash into some gigantic self-aggrandising project, he could have been sued by minority shareholders. (This did in fact happen, when the Dodge brothers took him to court – but not until years later.) In short, had Ford really wanted to be a philanthropist we would have expected him to do his good works later in life, after seeking more publicity, and using his own money rather than the resources of his company.

Most tellingly, Ford himself repeatedly claimed that his aim with the five-dollar day was not philanthropic, it was to make money. This would have been an odd claim to make if he was trying to burnish his reputation as a do-gooder. Instead, Ford called the five-dollar day 'one of the finest cost cutting moves we ever made'.

Come on, then. Tell me how a needless wage increase can cut costs.

The answer comes from looking at Ford's turnover rates. In 1913, the year before the five-dollar day was introduced, the Ford plant had to hire over 50,000 workers – yet the factory itself employed only around 13,500 staff. Tens of thousands of men quit and had to be replaced. The average worker stuck around for just three months. In one single month – March 1913 – over seven thousand workers left the company for one reason or another, more than half the workforce. And most of these left in unpredictable fashion: as 'five-day men'. That was the term for people who simply didn't bother turning up at work five days running, and were then assumed to have resigned.

This high turnover was, however, a symptom of the underlying problem, not the problem itself. Turnover was probably disruptive, but not excessively so because new workers were easy to hire and could quickly be trained. The underlying problem was that Ford workers were so unhappy with the job. Hours were long, the job was tedious, wages were poor, and factory floor bosses were – according to an internal review document – annoying fools. (Nothing changes.) Workers therefore had a tendency to slack off, skip work without notice, quarrel with supervisors on the shop floor and perhaps even sabotage the production line by literally throwing a spanner in the works. When the economy was in decent shape it was easy to walk into a similar job in a different factory, so few workers would have cared a jot about being fired. This was not, you may surmise, a recipe for a well-functioning workplace.

Henry Ford was musing over this problem one day in 1912 with a fellow by the name of Percival Perry. Perry was in charge of Ford's Trafford Park factory in Manchester, the sole outpost of the Ford Motor Company in England. Perry told Ford that when the Trafford Park factory started operating, he had paid the going rate of about one and a half pounds a week. This was enough to recruit workers for the factory, but not enough for those workers to properly support a family. As a result, they were distracted by hunger and lacked motivation. So Perry decided to pay all workers £3 a week instead, double the going rate. He called this approach 'high wages and straight wages', and it greatly improved productivity. Ford listened to Perry explain all this – and then he went back to Detroit to apply much the same strategy.

Henry Ford's adoption of Perry's 'high wages and straight wages' policy did three things. First, it meant that workers had a better standard of living and were likely to be able to maintain a stable family home and feed themselves well; with Ford's sociology department on the case, they were unlikely to spend too much of the extra cash on booze. Second, workers might have felt a sense of gratitude and obligation to the Ford Motor Company, and therefore have applied themselves much more vigorously to the job of making cars. And third, Ford's five-dollar day meant that suddenly his workers had a lot to lose. The job they had at Ford paid twice what they could earn elsewhere. As a result they had every reason to work hard, look busy and follow instructions. One commentary of the day recorded that 'the workingmen are absolutely docile'.

Just as had happened at Trafford Park, the move was a great success. Workforce turnover plummeted, as you'd expect, but the real measure of success was dramatically increased labour productivity. Ford was paying his men more, but getting a great deal more out of them. The factory produced more cars, and profits – despite the recession – continued to rise.

Good for him. But none of this explains your line that Ford 'invented unemployment'.

Well, we started this chapter talking about the simple supply-and-demand view of unemployment, and in a sense Henry

Ford's pre-1914 setup was much like that. He was operating in a labour market that looked like something you might see described in the classical textbooks. In this kind of 'perfect' labour market, workers are interchangeable, employers are too, and wages settle at a 'prevailing rate' – in the words of Ford's rival – at which anyone who wants a job can find one. If, as a worker, you fancied a holiday, you could take one without notice, walking out of the factory and heading for the beach. (In the Ford jargon, you became a 'five-day man'.) When you returned, you simply found yourself a job at your old employer, or a different employer – it didn't matter which. Your old employer wouldn't have cared that you'd left, because he could easily hire another worker just like you at a moment's notice.

Now, there are still some markets today that function rather similarly – the market for self-employed taxi drivers, for instance – and there are some parts of the world where building labourers pick up work by the day at whatever the going rate is. But most real labour markets nowadays are startlingly unlike this: they require quite a lot of effort on the part of both the employer and the employee to get things started, company-specific experience and training will tend to come in very handy, and typically both parties to the employment contract will hope it lasts.

So the solution to the five-dollar-day mystery isn't just a business case study. It tells us something very significant about the wider economy. Because what Ford – or, rather, Perry – discovered is that when it comes to hiring workers, what makes a market operate perfectly is not necessarily what makes good business sense.

As soon as Ford instituted the five-dollar day, his workers

no longer lived in the perfectly functioning labour market of the classical textbooks, in which they could walk out of one job and into another at a moment's notice. They operated instead on the fortunate side of a highly imperfect labour market. Inside the factory walls were workers paid well above the market rate. Outside were queues of unemployed men, being hosed down in sub-freezing temperatures by the police. There was no difference between the outsiders and the insiders in terms of their skills or character or willingness to work; the insiders had merely been lucky in managing to secure great jobs and were understandably keen to keep them. The outsiders had merely been unlucky.

Economists call Percival Perry's 'straight wages and high wages' policy 'efficiency wages'. Efficiency wages are higher than the competitive market wages, but nevertheless make good commercial sense for all the reasons we've discussed. Efficiency wages are good for many people. They're good for employers, who secure a loyal and motivated workforce. And they're good for the workers who manage to get good jobs. But because efficiency wages are higher than the wage at which supply equals demand, there's a problem: employers, with more productive (but more expensive) workers, will tend to employ fewer people; meanwhile, because higher wages and better conditions are on offer, more people will want to work. This is where the basic idea of supply and demand does come in useful again: it correctly predicts that efficiency wages, for all their commercial logic, mean we will have more job-hunters and fewer jobs.

So that's the sense in which I semi-jokingly said that Henry Ford invented unemployment. Of course unemployment was with us long before Ford came along, but Ford's system introduced a new and important source of unemployment. By pioneering efficiency wages, he helped to bring into existence a group of people who want to work but, through sheer bad luck, can't find jobs. You should bear that in mind the next time someone tells you the unemployed are all workshy layabouts.

I see. So if unemployment is a matter of sheer bad luck, then it would be only fair to offer generous welfare benefits to the unemployed. Right?

Ah. Well – hold on a moment. Having said that we shouldn't condemn the unemployed as workshy layabouts, we also have to recognise human nature. Unemployment benefits are effectively paying people to be unemployed. And if you raise the pay for people who don't work, then you have to expect that more unemployed people will be tempted to put a bit less effort into looking for work.

Both of these factors – efficiency wages and unemployment benefits – contribute to something we economists call 'structural unemployment'. Everyone associates unemployment with recessions, and of course in recessions we tend to see more workers being laid off and fewer being hired. But structural unemployment is the unemployment that's always there, even when the economy's booming – these are people who can't get Ford-style jobs because wages are deliberately kept high (or sometimes because minimum-wage laws have set the legal minimum too high), and people who decide that a life on benefits is preferable to a life of hard work – or, at least, that it makes sense to take a few months on benefits to look for a job they want, rather than simply taking the first job that happens to be available.

So how can I tell whether people are unemployed because of a recession, or because of these structural reasons?

With difficulty, naturally. But one helpful tool is the 'Beveridge curve', named after the architect of the UK's post-war welfare state, the economist William Beveridge. This plots the number of vacancies being advertised against the unemployment rate. It's a negative correlation: the more vacancies there are, the lower the unemployment rate will tend to be. Imagine a curved line running from the top left of a graph (lots of vacancies, low unemployment – the economy is booming) to the bottom right (few vacancies, high unemployment – a recession). If you measure the vacancy rate and unemployment rate of a particular economy at any time, the result will be a point on that economy's Beveridge curve at that particular time.

When the economy goes into recession, or recovers, we'd expect the data to move along the line – up towards the top left in the good times, down towards the bottom right in bad times. But if something happens to affect structural unemployment, we'd expect the data to move off the line entirely: the Beveridge curve itself would be moving. Let's say, for example, that you decide to pay extremely lavish benefits to the unemployed. We'd expect this to shift the entire curve out to the right. From now on, however well the economy is doing, the unemployment rate will be higher than it would have been. More vacancies will still be associated with lower unemployment, but for any given vacancy rate, the unemployment rate will now be higher. That is a structural problem with the economy, and it shows up in a higher Beveridge curve.

Let me give you an example of the difference between a move along the Beveridge curve and a shift of the entire curve. In the US, before the recession of 2008, unemployment had been less than 5 per cent. It quickly rose to 10 per cent in the autumn of 2009, as recession kicked in. This is a standard move along the Beveridge curve. By 2012, the economy was showing definite signs of recovery – more and more vacancies were being advertised. But instead of moving back up the previous curve towards the top left of the graph, the unemployment rate stayed stubbornly high, barely falling below 8 per cent. This wasn't a move back up the old Beveridge curve. Instead it produced a new, higher curve. In other words, it suggested that much of this unemployment might have been structural, rather than cyclical. If true – and it is a little early to tell – that will be bad news for the US. However well the economy is doing, unemployment is going to be higher now than it would have been. And that lamentable state of affairs will continue until another structural shift lowers the Beveridge curve once again.

If you look across developed countries, you'll find very different Beveridge curves – that is, levels of structural unemployment. The unemployment rate when economic times are good is typically about 3 per cent in Korea and Iceland, for instance, 5 per cent in the UK, 10 per cent in Germany, and 15 per cent in Poland. The average across the

European Union is about 8.5 per cent, and across the Organisation for Economic Cooperation and Development (OECD), a club of rich nations, it's about 6.5 per cent. If you want to know how to get unemployment down, it's not enough to be interested in how to solve recessions – you also have to ask why structural unemployment varies so much across different economies.

Economists have concluded that part of the answer has to do with dating.

Dating? As in, looking for a partner?

Yes. Think of it this way – when you're unemployed, we say you're a 'job-hunter', or that you're 'looking for work'. And those phrases are pretty reasonable descriptions of what's going on. You don't sell your labour in the way that a supermarket sells tomatoes. A supermarket doesn't describe itself as 'hunting for customers': the customers are out there and if the price and quality are right, the customers will buy. But job hunting isn't like that at all: you don't simply say, 'My labour is for sale and the quality is decent – I wonder at what price the job customer will choose to buy.' You take your time and look around until you find a job that seems right for you.

Nor do would-be employers simply advertise a job at a certain wage without caring who turns up. They're hunting, too. In most lines of work, employers have to spend some time and effort advertising the existence of vacancies and working out which applicants are right for the job. For some jobs the recruitment process is extraordinarily time-consuming and expensive.

For many years, this practical reality was brushed under the carpet by economic theorists – it seemed to add a lot of complexity to the analysis without adding a great deal of insight. But we've begun to realise that explicitly modelling the process of job search and recruitment is valuable. Unemployment is now routinely modelled as a process of searching for a match between a suitable vacancy and a suitable worker, much like dating and marriage. Christopher Pissarides won a Nobel prize for his work on this topic.[3] He points out that unemployment is the initial condition of economic existence, just as being single is the initial condition of romantic existence – all of us are born unemployed and single, and if we want that situation to change, sooner or later we will have to start looking for a suitable match.

These 'search' models of unemployment have proved very useful in understanding the problem. They help us to solve the puzzle that – according to the supply-and-demand school of thought – unemployment initially appears to be. And they point towards some strategies we might use to try to tackle the structural element of unemployment – in other words, to shift the Beveridge curve to the left. If there's a way to shift the Beveridge curve in that direction, this is pretty much a free lunch: you get lower unemployment whether your economy is booming or in a slump.

So how do I get my free lunch?

A few suggestions.

The first is to subsidise this matching process, especially for young people. (Yes, I realise a subsidy isn't quite a free lunch but it could potentially be excellent value.) It's particularly a problem for them because they don't have a lot of experience of job hunting. They don't have many contacts. They don't know a lot about what kind of job might suit them, and because they have no track record, they will find it hard to prove to employers that they're worth taking a chance on.

We don't need to subsidise young people to date, because they seem to enjoy that particular process of working out whether there's a suitable match or not. But if you're talking about a young person applying for a job she might not like and might not have much aptitude for, you can see that employers might not be terribly keen to spend a lot of money on training her. The problem is that when young job-seekers get training, they are more likely to end up applying for appropriate jobs, which is good for employers; also, a particular employer might end up training somebody only to find them leaving for a competitor. For all these reasons the social benefit of job training is quite likely to be larger than the benefit for any given individual – a good argument in favour of some kind of subsidy. (Attentive readers of *The Undercover Economist* will recognise that this is a case of positive externalities: nice spill-over effects that don't happen as much as they should.)

It's not like an economist to propose a subsidy.

No. It isn't. So these subsidies need to be tested properly. As an example, consider the Future Jobs Fund (FJF), which ran for a couple of years in the UK. The basic idea was pretty crude: the government paid employers £150 a week – very roughly $250 or €200 – to hire a young person for six months, plus a couple of thousand pounds up front. There were some restrictions: the new job was supposed to be a job that would not otherwise have existed, for instance, and it was supposed to provide a community benefit. But if you believe such restrictions mean terribly much, I'd like to sell you Tower Bridge.

Naturally, such substantial subsidies did persuade employers to hire lots of young people, at least while the subsidies lasted. Many of the young workers were sacked again at the end of the six months. The Future Jobs Fund was shut down early in 2011; the government was unconvinced that such crude subsidies would deliver any lasting benefits.

Rather splendidly, though, the relevant government department had commissioned a study of the long-term benefits of the programme, which was peer-reviewed and published in the autumn of 2012, over a year after the Fund had been terminated. A proper randomised trial wasn't conducted, but the analysis is fairly solid. The conclusion of the study, which tried to compare programme participants with otherwise identical non-participants, was that two years after starting the FJF programme, participants were 11 percentage points more likely to be in proper, non-subsidised jobs; they were 7 percentage points less likely to be claiming welfare benefits. These benefits were felt long after the six-month programme itself had finished, of course. The total net benefits of the programme to participants, employers and society as a whole were estimated at about £18,000 per participant, roughly evenly split between the three; to achieve this result the government had to spend a net £3100 per participant. It was an extraordinarily effective programme – what a shame it was shut down before the evaluation had been completed.[4]

Following the same logic, we could also try subsidising agencies that match workers to jobs – although I would like to see that sort of thing carefully piloted and tested, too, because promising-sounding ideas often fail in practice. For instance, there was recently a large study in France conducted by a team including Esther Duflo, one of the leaders in the use of field experiments. The study was evaluating what seemed a reasonable way to help people find jobs. Many job seekers in France are eligible for some career counselling to help them find a job, but this experiment chose some of them, at random, to receive extra intensive advice from a private firm, for up to a year, to help them find work.[5]

This kind of experiment is essential if we're to figure out how to make better public policy. But in this case, the experiment told us something useful but depressing: the intensive career counselling didn't work well. The uptake was low, the effect was small and temporary, and worst of all, the counselling didn't help the job market as a whole to work better, it simply gave those who received it a small competitive edge. While they were slightly more likely to find work, their peers who (at random) did not receive the counselling became less likely to find work, presumably because the competition had become slightly stiffer.

The next thing we can do is make it easier for people to move in search of work. Many of the policies that governments favour tend to militate against that. In the UK, for instance, it's hard to get permission to build houses near where jobs are being created. It's also expensive to move house, if you own one; while owning and living in a house is a tax-free affair, actually buying a house attracts a large one-off tax bill. In the US, owning a house is heavily subsidised through the mortgage interest deduction, which means that people with mortgages pay less tax. And if a region is struggling, the political instinct is always to try to reanimate the dying, rather than support the birth of something new, so declining regions tend to attract subsidies, which encourage people to stay rather than to move on to a more vibrant location where work may be easier to find. For all these reasons, economies will often have lots of vacancies in one region while there is high unemployment in another.

There are other good reasons why people don't want to move away from friends and family.

Yes, there are. But we need to recognise that encouraging people to put down roots isn't an unadulterated good. There are costs to it as well as benefits.

Speaking of benefits, where do welfare benefits fit in here?

I think the general story is quite clear: if you give people more generous benefits when they are out of work, they will be less desperate to do what it takes to find work. Other things being equal, generous benefits will tend to push the Beveridge curve out, meaning that for any given level of vacancies there will be more unemployment. One possible explanation for the fact that the Beveridge curve seems to be drifting out in the US is that unemployment insurance has been extended. Another possible explanation, following on from what I was saying about moving to find work, is the troubles of the housing market – people have become trapped by falling house prices, unable to sell up and pay off their mortgages. This makes it more difficult to relocate.

There is an argument that more generous welfare benefits might actually create more lasting, valuable jobs in the long run, because they allow people the breathing space to find a job that really suits their skills and interests. But the main argument in favour of such benefits is the humane one: even if they do tend to push up unemployment, that is a price worth paying to live in a civilised society.

So: subsidise job hunting, make relocating easier, and pitch unemployment benefit at a level that's humane but not excessive. And that will do the trick?

Well, it should help. But you'll not be surprised to hear that there's no single answer. Two countries which have historically had rather low structural unemployment, Germany and the US, take very different approaches. Germany has an elaborate system of apprenticeships and training to get young people into jobs, and also subsidises the self-employed, which helps keep people working and improving their skills. The US system takes a very different approach: it's ultra-flexible. People can be dismissed on a whim, which can't be much fun.

But the advantage, of course, is that people can also be hired on a whim. As a result it's easier to get a foot on the employment ladder. Different systems, different advantages and disadvantages.

What's pretty clear is what doesn't work: the Mediterranean model of Spain, Italy and Greece provides little help to young people and extravagant protection to people with permanent contracts. In Spain, the standard employment contract provides forty-five days' redundancy pay per year of service. For every eight years working for a company, then, you get a year's pay if they sack you. The result is a sclerotic labour market: because it is almost impossible to sack well-established workers, companies are extremely cautious about hiring. Unemployment rates are high.

While the problem is obvious, the solution isn't easy. It would take a bold politician to sweep away protections of established workers, so Spain tried a partial reform – many young workers now have a new form of temporary contract with very limited rights. Unfortunately, this has arguably made things worse. When a recession strikes, these young workers suffer the full force of the blow – no employer looking to cut costs in a recession would sack a permanent employee when there was a temporary one who could be fired first, no matter how capable that temporary employee might be. And naturally, the temporary employees tend to be passed over for training. Meanwhile the job-for-lifers can relax, knowing their jobs are very safe. They would also be unwise to move jobs, even if the job description changed and they became unhappy or incompetent, because they would be losing their carefully accrued job security. In short, the two-tier labour market is both inefficient and hugely unfair, giving Spain many of the disadvantages of a rigid labour market while somehow managing to grab the disadvantages of a flexible one, too. Youth unemployment rates have been hovering around 50 per cent during the Euro crisis and there is no sign of improvement as I write these words. The reform was supposed to be a useful first step, but Spain's policymakers now seem trapped with one foot on either side of a widening crevasse.[5]

OK. Time for a précis.

Fair enough. There are basically two types of unemployment: the cyclical employment that comes and goes as recessions come and go, and more permanent structural unemployment. Structural unemployment is a function of all sorts of things, some inevitable (some people will always be 'between jobs', however briefly) and some the unwelcome side-effect of policies such as unemployment benefits and minimum wages, and some as a result of Henry Ford-style efficiency wages. Structural unemployment need not be permanent – for instance, if it results in old industries shrinking while new industries grow, we would hope that people could retrain and find new jobs in due course. But structural unemployment, even if temporary, will not be helped much by demand-boosting stimulus policies.

There are two ways to fight unemployment. One is to fight recessions – constantly battling to get the economy to the top left of the Beveridge curve, with plenty of vacancies and few unemployed people. But the other is more structural, trying to shift the curve down and to the left, so that for any given level of vacancies, there will be fewer people without work. For the most part, I don't see any reason why you can't try both methods at the same time.

There's something else, though – something that often goes missing when economists discuss unemployment. And that's the study of management.

9

Boss-o-nomics

'What upsets me about the job? Wasted talent. People could come to me, and they could go, "Excuse me, David, but you've been in the business twelve years. Can you just spare us a moment to tell us how to run a team, how to keep them task-orientated as well as happy?" But they don't. That's the tragedy.'

David Brent, *The Office*

Surely it's obvious that management matters – David Brent and Michael Scott, the awful bosses in *The Office*, inadvertently prove that every day of their sad, fictional lives.

Of course. But while unemployment is generally regarded as a key concern for the economist, the frustrations of office life have not tended to be regarded as any of our business. As far as economic performance is concerned, management has been viewed as one of those exogenous things, like the supply of Red Cross parcels to a prison camp. Maybe management improves over time, and maybe it doesn't – either way, it's just not seemed to be the sort of thing an economist can sensibly discuss. Fortunately, that is now starting to change.[1]

What's enabled the change is that we now have better data. For a long time, we've known that there's been a puzzling discrepancy in the productivity of different firms within the same industry. Some scrape by, some go bankrupt, and some are hugely profitable and successful. It wouldn't be a huge surprise to hear that good and bad management played an important part in explaining that trend. The difficulty has been proving it. John van Reenen and Nick Bloom are members of a small group of economists who have started to do so, taking management seriously as an explanation for why some economies work well and others do not. Van Reenen and Bloom have developed a large, carefully administered survey designed to measure management practices.

I sense a problem here. The likes of David Brent and Michael Scott are unlikely to give an honest and self-aware account of their management practices in a survey.

Indeed not. That's why the surveyors – confident, chatty MBA students with a reasonable amount of business experience themselves – arrange to conduct long, open-ended telephone interviews with middle managers in the firms that are being surveyed. (These interviews are long enough and open-ended enough that the interviewees have been known to attempt to chat up the interviewers, in ways that revealed intriguing cultural differences. In the UK, a British manager said to his Australian interviewer, 'Your accent is really cute and I love the way you talk. Do you fancy meeting up near the factory?' The response, alas, was: 'Sorry, but I'm washing my hair every night for the next month.' In India the conversation was a little different: 'Are you a Brahmin?' 'Yes, why do you ask?' 'And are you married?' 'No.' 'Excellent, excellent, my son is looking for a bride and I think you could be perfect. I must contact your parents to discuss this.')

When not fending off romantic advances, the interviewers are ostensibly conducting an interview about 'lean management practices' – that is, the way the firm operates, rather than any financial details. And the interview is conducted double-blind: the surveyors don't know anything about the financial performance of the company they are assessing, while the managers who are being interviewed don't know that what they say is being carefully marked against a variety of specific criteria. The questions are designed to discover what goes on inside a company without offering a menu of answers, which might introduce a bias. Instead of asking, for instance, 'Do you promote on merit?', the interviewer would say, 'Imagine that a worker had been with you for a year. How would you go about considering whether he or she should be promoted?' Over the course of many such questions the interviewers can assess the quality of different management practices.

By the end of 2010, the team had completed over eight thousand of these interviews, spotting businesses with sloppy inventory management, promotion based purely on tenure, a failure to monitor performance, and other Stone Age management techniques.

The upshot? As you'd expect, management quality seems to matter a lot. It's very closely correlated with labour productivity, and labour productivity is, in the long run, about as important a number as exists in an economy – it explains why a typical Tanzanian worker produces in a month what an

American worker produces in a day, even given the same equipment. We can't prove that better management is responsible for the entire gap, but it seems highly likely to be part of the story.

So, I'm curious – which countries have the worst managers?

That's such a negative way of asking the question – but if you insist, it's India, followed by China, Brazil and Greece. I should say that those are the worst performers of a list of twenty, most of which are rich countries. China, Brazil and India presumably were thought worth examining because they're such large, important economies.

The US has the best management in the world, according to Bloom and van Reenen. Japan, Germany, Sweden and Canada are in a little group behind the US, and the next group down includes Australia, the UK, Italy and France.

That's interesting, but is it useful to me in my position of supreme economic dictator? I can hardly wander up and down the country finding Pointy-Haired Bosses and giving them wedgies, can I?

No, you can't. And I wouldn't send the civil service to do it for you, either, because – according to Bloom and van Reenen – government-run companies are right at the bottom of management-quality tables.

But there are things you can do.

It turns out that the difference between, say, the United States and India isn't that the best US firms are better run than the best Indian firms. Instead, it's that the Indian economy is host to a lot of really badly managed companies; these are much scarcer in the United States. The way to improve average management performance is either to force those firms to raise their game, or to replace them with something better. And there's a handy tool to achieve both those aims: it's called competition. Badly managed companies struggle to survive if they have decent competitors, so promote competition and you'll raise management standards. And the way to promote competition is to do pretty much the opposite of what India has done for so long – what you need is to break up large monopolists, reduce the red tape that slows down startups, improve transport infrastructure so that companies can compete outside their home town, and be open to global competitors.

In a recent study published in the *Journal of Financial Economics*, Kathy Fogel, Randall Morck and Bernard Yeung compiled lists of the ten largest employers in forty-four countries across the world.[2] They found that countries with rapid churn into and out of this elite set of employers also had faster-growing economies. More impressively, this relationship appears to be causal – high turnover yesterday is correlated with fast economic growth tomorrow – and holds up after statistically controlling for other important factors. Fogel and her colleagues also argue that the key factor is not 'rising stars' but 'disappearing behemoths'. Corporate failure is often mistakenly associated with the failure of an economy as a whole, and of course a recession will put companies out of business. But corporate failure isn't the cause of economic trouble – it's the process by which badly managed companies are replaced by more productive competitors. To put it another way, you can't have success without embracing some individual failures on the way. And if I may be forgiven for a brief plug, that's the theme of my last book, *Adapt*.

All right, all right. You're supposed to be telling me how to run my economy. Is it possible for me somehow to improve management practice more directly?

Well, you could certainly try to avoid actively undermining good management. Here's an example from the UK: if you pass the family business on to your children when you die, it will be free of inheritance tax. John van Reenen points out that this is a tax incentive to keep a company inside the family, and in the UK it remains quite common to hand the reins of the family firm over to the eldest son – a man who may be entirely unsuited to the task. Van Reenen's research says that family-managed firms tend to be poorly managed firms.

Or maybe you could be even more direct, and send in the management consultants.

Ha! Yes, a few sharply dressed Harvard Business School graduates with no relevant experience should do the trick.

You laugh, but actually there is some evidence on management consultants – and it is from India, the world's leading practitioner of bad management.

Accenture, a large management consulting firm, agreed to subject its advice to a randomised trial. The partners must have balls of steel – or perhaps they didn't realise what they were letting themselves in for. After all, the study – conducted by a team of economists at the World Bank, Berkeley and Stanford, and including Nick Bloom – was ostensibly about whether modern management techniques would improve the productivity of large textile firms in India. But naturally, if you want to improve management techniques, you send in a management consulting firm, so the study also became a test of Accenture's advice.

The researchers hired Accenture, at a discounted rate, to provide management consulting services to a group of factories in Tarapur and Umbergaon – two textile manufacturing centres about an hour north of Mumbai. The researchers approached sixty-six Indian firms to ask if they'd be interested in receiving a quarter of a million dollars' worth of free management consulting – Stanford and the World Bank were paying Accenture's fees, so the factory owners themselves didn't have to pay anything. The fact that most of them said 'no' tells you something about the attitudes of Indian managers and the reputation of management consultants.

Eventually, twenty factories were selected to participate in the study and, at random, fourteen were chosen to receive the full consulting service (a month's diagnostic work followed by four months of management advice) while the other six were a control group, who received the one-month performance audit, but little serious advice.

The results were undeniably impressive. The effect of a few months of consulting advice was to raise profits by almost a fifth, to the tune of several hundred thousand dollars a year.

Output was up, inventory was tighter, and defect rates were halved.

Accenture's fees for the five-month consulting gig, at commercial rates, would have been roughly the same amount as the increase in profits – so the arrangement would have paid for itself by the end of the year. If any of the consulting advice stuck, this would have been a fantastic investment. The indications are that the advice more than sticks: the new procedures generate more information, more ideas for running a tight ship, and a spiral of continuous improvement.

Before we all rush out to hire a management consultant, two notes of caution. The first is that as the experiment was actually designed to evaluate management techniques rather than management consultants, Accenture were left in charge of collecting their own performance data. (The data was subject to some independent checking, however, and there is no evidence that anything was amiss.)

The more substantial caveat is that textile firms in India have their own distinct problems: tools and machinery were left lying around, and stock control was frequently non-existent. If a worker needed to find a particular item, the technique of choice was simply to forage around in the storage bins until something useful emerged. The store-room might be locked, with the sole key hanging around the neck of the factory owner – a security measure that could cause hours of delays. There were, to put it mildly, some low-hanging fruits for the management consultants to pick. Modern inventory-management techniques made a big difference in this particular sector of Mumbai's economy, but that does not mean that Tesco or Apple – or even the civil service – has as much to gain from bringing the consultants in.

You mean I don't have to completely surrender my cynicism about sharply dressed Harvard Business School graduates with no relevant experience?

It would be nice to know whether management consultants could prove their worth in London or New York. I don't know the answer, though I do know some economists who would happily supervise a randomised trial.

But put it this way: I would focus on promoting competition, not bringing in the consultants. Many industries are cosily protected against competitors, one way or another, and competitive pressure is a good way to improve management quality – as well, incidentally, as lowering prices, increasing demand for skilled workers, and promoting innovation.

10

The sirens of macroeconomics

'When it is detonated, it will produce enough lethal radioactive fallout so that within ten months, the surface of the Earth will be as dead as the moon! ... It is not a thing a sane man would do. The Doomsday Machine is designed to trigger itself automatically.'

Soviet Ambassador Sadeski, in *Dr Strangelove, or How I Learned to Stop Worrying and Love the Bomb*

Why are you quoting a nuclear annihilation comedy in a book about economics?

It'll be helpful in understanding why you probably should have an independent central bank, why you probably shouldn't extend that model to too many other parts of your economic management, and why the euro crisis happened. This chapter is all about credibility – why it matters, and why it's also inherently risky.

That seems an unlikely amount of economic explanatory power for a cult 1960s movie.

I'll have you know that one of the true economic greats, Thomas Schelling, advised Stanley Kubrick when he was working on the script for *Dr Strangelove*. In fact it was talking to Schelling that persuaded Kubrick that the film had to be a black comedy rather than a thriller: Schelling convinced him that there were, thankfully, few realistic scenarios in which a total nuclear war would result.

Schelling was originally a trade negotiator; he worked on the Marshall Plan, hammering out the terms of US aid to Europe after the Second World War. He became fascinated by the moves and counter-moves of a well-thought-out negotiation, and by the uses and abuses of game theory, a newly developed mathematical approach to modelling interactions between competing sides. In the late 1950s, Schelling took both his policy perspectives and a cautious affection for game theory into the field of nuclear deterrence. He became an influential thinker on the subject, usually at one remove through colleagues and protégés who advised John F. Kennedy, Robert McNamara and Henry Kissinger through the Berlin crisis, the Cuban missile crisis and the Vietnam War.

One of Schelling's most striking ideas, which formed the basis of the plot of *Dr Strangelove*, was the commitment strategy: the idea that by limiting your own options you might actually gain an advantage, because of the effect that might have on your opponent's decision-making. A simple example is the policy in banks and armoured cars that the front-line staff don't have access to the safe. If bank robbers know that the staff can't open the safe, there is not much point in threatening the staff and insisting that they try.

The Doomsday Machine, as imagined in *Dr Strangelove*, was the ultimate commitment strategy – a set of bombs vast enough to destroy all life and render the atmosphere toxically radioactive 'for ninety-three years', which is designed to be triggered automatically in the event of a nuclear attack on the Soviet Union (or if anyone attempts to disarm it). The commitment strategy lies in this automatic trigger. As Ambassador Sadeski points out, 'only a madman' would trigger the Doomsday Machine voluntarily, so the threat to do so wouldn't be believable. But the trigger makes a perfect deterrent – nobody would ever attack the Soviet Union once it had built a Doomsday Machine. As Dr Strangelove himself comments, 'Deterrence is the art of producing in the mind of the enemy the fear to attack. And so because of the automated and irrevocable decision-making process which rules out human meddling, the Doomsday Machine is terrifying, simple to understand, and completely credible and convincing.'

Schelling developed the idea of commitment strategies in all kinds of different realms, including battles of will with your own demons – making a bet with a friend, for example, could help you to stop smoking. When Schelling was working through these ideas in the 1960s, they had no obvious implications for macroeconomics. But in the 1970s, amidst the economic chaos of the oil shocks, the conversation changed radically. Schelling's idea of credible commitment now shapes most of our major economic institutions, not always for the better.

To begin this story we need to go back to Bill Phillips.

The man who invented the MONIAC.

The very same. After the triumph of the MONIAC, and despite lacking serious qualifications, in 1950 Phillips was appointed as a lecturer at the London School of Economics. He was given the maximum allowable salary, and put on the fast track to a professorship while studying for his Ph.D. Phillips had a stellar reputation in the department. Lionel Robbins, the departmental head, wrote in an internal memo that Phillips was on the verge of making the most important contribution since John Maynard Keynes's book *A General Theory of Employment, Interest and Money*, published twenty years before. And yet, in academia, one must publish or perish: Phillips badly needed to get some publications under his belt if the department were to justify making him a professor.

Ever since constructing the MONIAC, Bill Phillips had been fascinated by the dynamics of the economic system – the way it fluctuated or even oscillated like a pendulum, and the way those fluctuations might be damped down. It was a natural question for an engineer to ask, although it remains a fiendish problem for economists even today. As part of his work on economic dynamics, Phillips gathered data on nominal wages (a good proxy for inflation) and on unemployment, and plotted the data on a graph. He found a strong and surprisingly precise empirical relationship between the two: when nominal wages were rising strongly, unemployment would tend to be low. When nominal wages were falling or stagnant, unemployment would be high.

Phillips himself seems not to have been especially awed by this discovery, which he put together over the course of a weekend. He put it to one side to continue his deeper and more sophisticated theoretical work on damping down economic oscillations. Bill Phillips was in no hurry: he was a man who liked to think profoundly and to think differently. But his colleagues were becoming agitated that their campaign to award him a professorial chair would be derailed by his diffident approach to publishing. And if the LSE establishment blocked his appointment, the man his colleagues regarded as a genius might leave for Australia or America.

So Phillips, under pressure from his colleagues to publish something, dusted off his weekend's work and turned it into a paper. He was unimpressed with his own work, later describing it as 'a rushed job'. Bill's colleagues, ever eager to help his career along, got the paper published in the LSE's journal, *Economica*, under the title 'The Relationship between Unemployment and the Rate of Change of Money Wages in the United Kingdom 1861–1957'. And it became the most cited academic paper in the history of macroeconomics.[1]

Really? It doesn't seem that surprising a result – rising wages means lower unemployment.

That's what Bill himself thought. The reason the 'Phillips curve' became so popular is that other economists – notably Paul Samuelson – championed the idea that policymakers could pick a point on the curve to aim for. If they wanted to reduce unemployment, they'd have to tolerate higher inflation; if they wanted to get inflation down, they'd have to accept higher unemployment. They could look at the curve, decide what trade-off between inflation and unemployment they were willing to tolerate, and set their monetary policy accordingly.

Sounds reasonable.

It does. But, unfortunately, it doesn't work. It turns out that saying, 'High inflation has always been correlated with low unemployment, so we can tackle unemployment by accepting higher inflation' is a bit like saying, 'Fort Knox has never been robbed, so we can save money by sacking the guards.' You can't look just at the empirical data, you need also to think about incentives. High inflation has tended to mean lower unemployment because employers and job-seekers expected a particular rate of inflation and were occasionally surprised by a surge in prices; employers mistook it for increased demand and tried to hire workers, workers thought that they were being offered higher real wages. Both were mistaken: in fact what was really happening was that the economy was suffering unexpected inflation and they'd been slow to notice.

The problem was that people wouldn't keep on being surprised by inflation if policymakers, beguiled by the Phillips curve, kept deliberately creating inflation with the aim of suppressing unemployment. Nobody would be fooled; they would see the inflation coming a mile off. Inflation would rise but unemployment would not fall.

So when did this logic become apparent?

Samuelson's interpretation of the Phillips curve, as a kind of menu from which policymakers could pick their favourite combination of inflation and unemployment, was shattered by two blows, one empirical and one theoretical. The empirical blow came with the oil shocks of the 1970s, when inflation took off while unemployment remained stubbornly high. The clean lines of the Phillips curve disappeared in a tangle of stagflation. The theoretical attack came from a man called Robert Lucas. What became known as 'the Lucas critique' is going to be hugely important – and frustrating for you – as you try to keep your economy on track.

It's the Lucas critique that we've been discussing with all our talk of Fort Knox and incentives. Lucas wasn't the first to muse that the Phillips curve might dissolve if too much policy weight was placed on it. Milton Friedman and Edmund Phelps, both later to win the Nobel memorial prize in economics, had each put forward versions of that argument in the late 1960s. But Lucas had more influence in the end – perhaps because the Phillips curve was dissolving as he wrote, and perhaps because he pushed the arguments of Phelps and Friedman to their logical extreme. It wasn't just the Phillips curve that was a problem, said Lucas: it was any correlation between economic variables. These correlations didn't just emerge from a policy alone, but from the way individual decision-makers reacted to that policy. If you changed the policy then people would respond, and the correlation would change.

Here's an example of the Lucas critique, inspired by the economist Thomas Sargent: in American football (or 'football', as they so quaintly call it in the US), teams get four turns, called downs, to carry or pass the ball forward ten yards. Failing that, the other team takes possession. On the fourth down, it's common for teams to punt, kicking the ball far into the opposition's territory, even though this concedes possession.[2]

Now imagine that the sport's ruling body decides it wants to reduce punting in the game. The football bosses take a look at the statistical evidence and conclude that it's totally unambiguous: teams often punt on the fourth down and rarely punt at other times, so if the fourth down was simply abolished, punting would become extremely rare.

You can see the fault in the reasoning very easily if you stop looking at the empirical data, and start thinking about the incentives of the football team. They want to keep possession, but if losing it seems likely, they'd rather the ball was deep in the opposing half. When fourth down comes around, the team is about to lose possession anyway so they punt downfield. If the rule was changed to allow only three downs, they'd punt on the third down instead.

In the case of American football, the problem with the 'abolish the fourth down' rule is utterly obvious. But the analogous argument with economic policy and economic data hadn't been fully appreciated until Lucas came along. He punctured the hubris of the economics profession in the 1950s and 1960s. Economists had tended to assume that as their data got better and better, they would acquire a more and more reliable understanding of the world and they could use that understanding to run economies and prevent recessions. What Lucas showed was that the relationships economists were looking at – between inflation, unemployment, GDP growth and so on – weren't iron laws of economics. They could change. The data alone couldn't be trusted.

Slightly pessimistic, isn't it?

Yes, Lucas's idea did introduce an important undercurrent of nihilism into economics. Economists lost confidence in what they could learn from looking at empirical macroeconomic relationships. And if you can't trust the data, what can you trust? The answer is to turn to theory, using microeconomics to explicitly model how individuals reach their decisions. The problem is that the micro-founded modelling tended to bear little relationship to real economic data.

How can you justify ignoring the data?

I agree: you can't justify ignoring the data. But you can appreciate where economists were coming from, after the collapse of the Phillips curve and the irrefutable logic of the Lucas critique: if apparently rock-solid economic data dissolve when we try to build something on them, why should we care so much about whether economic models fit the data? The data didn't seem to be able to tell us anything about practical policy.

So the strategy, instead, was to develop economic models built on microeconomic ideas. That means thinking explicitly about individual incentives and expectations, rather than looking at broad swaths of macroeconomic data without a sense of the causal relationships. The hope was that those models would become sophisticated enough to explain real-world data, while being robust to changes in policy. But that might only happen later, perhaps decades later – and as Keynes reminded us, 'in the long run we're all dead'.

So how do these micro-founded models work?

They're based on an idea called 'rational expectations'. In its purest form, this theory is clearly unrealistic – it assumes that everybody being described in an economic model under-stands the model and will act rationally in accordance with their best interests. In the real world, people do not always act rationally and they don't understand the structure of the global economy – nobody understands that. Still, there's something to the rational expectations idea. People aren't complete chumps. If they keep hearing on the news that the government's policies are likely to lead to higher inflation in the future, at least some of them are likely to factor that into their decisions about how much of a wage rise to demand. And while it seems unreasonable to assume rational expec-tations, so far the economics profession has struggled to find a better alternative. Before Lucas, economists often didn't think much about expectations at all. At best they would assume that people simply thought the rate of inflation tomorrow would be the same as the rate of inflation today. An alternative idea was 'adaptive expectations', which would slowly adjust as reality itself adjusted. None of these alter-natives were very convincing.

Now, let's reconnect this story with Thomas Schelling and the idea of credibility. Robert Lucas told the economics profession to stop thinking about the economy like an engineering problem, with a single actor – the government – using fiscal and monetary policy to stabilise fluctuations in the economic system. Instead, we should think of the economy as being like a game, in which the government isn't the only player. And there is an analytical tool developed quite explicitly to deal with multi-player problems: it's game theory.

It wasn't long, then, before two economists – Finn Kydland and Edward Prescott – picked up Lucas's critique and began to apply game theory to the vast game of macroeconomics. They concluded straight away that credibility was a key issue. If people behave differently when they expect high inflation, the obvious lesson is that we need to persuade them to expect low inflation. But merely saying, 'We have a policy of low inflation' is like the Soviet Union saying, 'We have a policy of responding to any nuclear attack by letting off enough bombs to make the world uninhabitable.' Talk is cheap.

Before Friedman, Phelps and Lucas, economists assumed that the general public would play the role of Charlie Brown while the government acted like Lucy holding her football in a *Peanuts* cartoon: the public would charge up to kick the ball (agree low wage settlements) and then the government would whip the football away (create inflation). That story made no sense after the Lucas critique. The public wouldn't be Charlie Brown; they wouldn't believe the government's promises of low inflation.

If there is no credible reason for people to believe the government's promises, they will ignore what the government says and they will agree prices and wages in the confident expectation that inflation will actually be high. As a result, we get the worst of both worlds: high inflation, yet high unemployment, too. This unhappy combination characterised the 1970s, and came to be known as stagflation – stubbornly high inflation in a stagnating economy.

Which brings us back to Schelling and the idea of a commitment strategy. If the government could somehow make the promise of low inflation believable, everyone would be better off.

Yes. If you have a Doomsday Machine then you won't need to use it. And if you could put monetary policy 'on automatic', keeping inflation low even when it was tempting to print money, you could get the same output as in your non-credible world, but with lower inflation.

Excellent. Another free lunch! So what's the economic equivalent of the Doomsday Machine?

I am not sure that the words 'free lunch' and 'Doomsday Machine' should be so casually juxtaposed. But I have an answer: the economic equivalent of the Doomsday Machine is an independent central bank with a commitment to low inflation. Before Kydland and Prescott, only one such central bank existed in a major economy: West Germany's Bundesbank, established in 1957, bolstered by the traumatic folk memory of the Weimar hyperinflation and the rise of Hitler, and fiercely determined to keep a lid on inflation from day one.

After Kydland and Prescott – and of course, after the painful stagflation of the 1970s – other central banks began to think hard about credibility, too. The US Federal Reserve was already independent, but its chairman Paul Volcker demonstrated his determination to cause a deep recession in the cause of getting inflation down. In doing so he established the Federal Reserve's inflation-fighting credentials.

Other countries lacked independent central banks at all; monetary policy was easily controlled by finance ministers with an eye on the next election. But as the credibility issue became better understood, one by one the major economies granted independence to their central banks. Volcker and the Bundesbank provided the practical example; Kydland and Prescott provided the intellectual justification. The first of the new independent central banks was established in New Zealand, in 1989. In the UK and Japan it was 1997. The euro area acquired a central bank in 1999, before it even acquired a physical currency.

Lacking the reputation of a Bundesbank, these newly independent central banks typically acquired their credibility through a publicly announced inflation target. The Bank of England's is 2 per cent. In principle, the government of the day can change that target at any time. In practice, the political costs of fiddling with the inflation target seem to be prohibitive – it has happened only once. (Even then the target was moved down, not up, and it was coupled with a switch to an EU-approved measure of inflation.) The inflation target in almost any economy you care to name is now pretty credible, thanks to these legislative changes, or the historical reputation of the central bank itself, or both.

This sounds promising. If credibility is such a big deal in monetary policy, can I apply the principle to solve other macroeconomic problems?

There are occasionally proposals for other economic commitment devices. For example, one that's often proposed is some kind of constitutional requirement that the government balances its budget every year. It sounds like a common-sense way of cutting off politicians' temptation to irresponsibly run up debt, but it would be a disaster: in the good times, when welfare benefits were low and the tax base was healthy, tax rates would plunge, over-stimulating an already booming economy; in the bad times, when unemployment benefit claims rose and the tax base was shrinking, tax rates would have to soar, or spending programmes be axed, just when the economy most needed a boost.

Not that, then. Anything else?

Credibility is most helpful for long-term problems. One example is the problem of affording state benefits in ageing societies. We've known for three decades that developed countries would face an increasing challenge in funding state pensions, because the number of people of pension age was growing sharply relative to the number of younger workers paying tax to support the system. Now, if you could find a credible way to say to young people, 'You aren't going to have state benefits when you're old,' perhaps you could persuade them to start saving for their own old age – and if they do, that means you won't have to worry as much about them needing state benefits.

However, making such a threat credible seems to be difficult. For example, in 1980 Margaret Thatcher's Conservative government had a go at tackling this problem by severing the traditional link between state pensions and average earnings – instead, pensions would keep pace only with inflation. Because wages tend to outstrip price rises over time, the policy was a rather elegant way to make pensions shrink gradually – the difference between average wages and inflation is small enough not to be terribly noticeable over a few years, but over twenty or thirty years it would add up to a lot. Anyone young enough to be worried would also be young enough to put money aside to top up the pension, thus reducing the need for future state benefits.

But people would do so only if they believed the policy to be credible – that is, if they believed that Thatcher's successors would also stick to the plan. They didn't believe it, and indeed it's not what happened. Subsequent governments first supplemented the pension with all manner of extra goodies – free television licences, payments for 'winter fuel' – and finally reverted to a system that links the pension to earnings, or inflation, or an arbitrary fixed increase, whichever is the most favourable to pensioners. What was arguably a sensible way to ease people into providing for their own retirement was largely undone by the fact that the reform wasn't credible over the long term.

Climate change is another area where we could badly use

some credibility. Many governments have adopted extremely strict forty-year targets for carbon dioxide emissions. If people believed the governments really meant to meet these targets, then they would presumably rush to invest in low-carbon infrastructure such as tidal power or nuclear power – and this investment, in turn, would help those targets to be met. But potential investors are understandably wary about whether the government really means it, or might change the rules as it finds convenient – especially since short-term targets seem to be much harder to hit.

Now, in theory you could respond to these credibility problems in the same way as for inflation. But is it really sensible to try to set up the equivalent of the Bank of England for pensions or carbon emissions? An independent carbon emissions authority, for example, would have to have vast powers to regulate and tax all facets of the energy system. Do you really think it's possible to delegate so much power to technocrats and yet remain a democrat?

You're saying that monetary policy is a special case.

I think it is, for a couple of reasons. First of all, while the business of conducting modern monetary policy is impenetrably opaque, the basic aim is not hard to express. This means monetary policy lends itself well to an easily understandable division between democrats and technocrats – the democratically elected government sets the inflation target, and then the technocrats manipulate interest rates and the money supply to ensure the target is hit. Second, low inflation tends to be a relatively uncontroversial aim – people may grumble when their mortgage rates go up, but they generally also agree that preventing high inflation is a good idea.

. That's not the case with the aim of dramatically reducing state benefits or overhauling the energy system. You can bet there would be huge popular demand for government to wrest back control of state pensions from technocrats who kept cutting them, or of energy policy from technocrats who kept slapping taxes on petrol. This would, of course, undermine the technocrats' long-term credibility, and remove the point of creating them in the first place.

There's an even more fundamental problem with commitment devices, though. The most sensible-seeming commitment device can go horribly wrong if its design is flawed. Remember what happens at the end of *Dr Strangelove*?

Armageddon, right?

Indeed. The Soviets' Doomsday Machine would surely have succeeded in deterring attacks, if it weren't for the fact that they decided to keep it a secret for a few days (as Ambassador Sadeski explains with solemnity, while a nuclear war is breaking out all around him, 'It was to be announced at the Party Congress on Monday. As you know, the Premier loves surprises'); with unfortunate timing, Brigadier General Jack D. Ripper, who is determined to stop 'the international communist conspiracy to sap and impurify all of our precious bodily fluids', takes it upon himself to drop a bomb. That is the problem with commitment devices: if something unexpected goes wrong and a crisis happens anyway, the commitment device guarantees that it will escalate into Armageddon.

Unfortunately we have an important parallel in economics: it's called the Eurozone.

With Greece in the role of Jack D. Ripper?

Something like that; Greece, or the investors who lent money to Greece. One of the central ideas behind the creation of the Eurozone – and certainly the reason that so many weaker economies wanted to join it – was that it allowed every country in Europe to acquire the unassailable credibility of the Bundesbank. As a result, these peripheral economies would gain ready access to cheap money.

Before the euro was created, international investors were hesitant to lend money to Greece and indeed many other non-German economies. The fear was that Greece would find itself in trouble, print money, and pay off the debt in devalued drachma. Both the Greek government and the Greek private sector faced higher interest rates as a result of this risk, which of course made it more expensive to get things done in Greece – to build infrastructure, put up a new building or start up a new business.

When Greece joined the euro, it bound itself to the monetary policy of the European Central Bank, a credible independent central bank with more than a whiff of the Bundesbank about it. (The ECB is located in Frankfurt, literally a five-minute stroll across the park from the Bundesbank. Politically, it is heavily influenced by its inflation-crushing neighbour.) Of course, the Greeks could have announced a policy of tying the drachma's exchange rate to the euro. Superficially the economics would have been the same. But a drachma–euro exchange rate peg wouldn't have been credible. It was purely for the sake of credibility that Greece instead decided to abolish the drachma altogether and join the euro, which had been deliberately designed with no mechanism for a country to withdraw. Perhaps the Greek politicians were thinking of one of their country's earliest heroes, Odysseus, binding himself to the mast so that he could listen to the beautiful song of the Sirens without being lured to his death. By binding themselves to the euro, Greek politicians hoped to reap the rewards of their credible commitment.

And for a while, the commitment worked exactly as they had hoped. Believing that devaluation was now impossible, international investors willingly lent money, in euros, to Greece and to other hitherto risky economies on the European periphery.

But perhaps the Greek politicians should have remembered what happens to Odysseus later in his voyage, when he finds himself sucked towards the gaping maw of Charybdis, a submerged sea monster. Odysseus escapes by leaping from his raft and holding on to a fig tree – which is possible, of course, only because he is no longer tied to a mast. Having reassured investors that it was impossible for them to print money and devalue their debts, the Greek government promptly ran up unsustainable debts anyway. When the banking crisis hit in 2008, they found themselves being sucked towards Charybdis's lair but with no obvious way of jumping ship.

It would be possible, of course, for the European Central Bank to print money to support Greece and other beleaguered countries. (Spain and Italy have been regarded as particularly deserving of a bit of support from the ECB, because they seem to be the victims of self-fulfilling pessimism on the part of bond investors: able to pay their debts if investors have confidence, but not able to pay their debts if investors panic.) But credibility is credibility: the Bundesbank-influenced ECB has consistently been grudging in its willingness to risk any kind of inflation, no matter how severe the crisis. That is, after all, what credibility looks like.

I should beware of building too many Doomsday Machines into my economy, then.

They have their place, and I'd certainly recommend an independent central bank. But proceed with caution. Greece is teaching us the lesson Ambassador Sadeski also learned the hard way – the price of credibility can be a painful lack of flexibility when something goes wrong.

11

The cult of GNP

'Too much and for too long, we seemed to have
surrendered personal excellence and community values in
the mere accumulation of material things. Our Gross
National Product, now, is over $800 billion a year, but
that Gross National Product – if we judge the United
States of America by that – that Gross National Product
counts air pollution and cigarette advertising, and
ambulances to clear our highways of carnage. It counts
special locks for our doors and the jails for the people who
break them. It counts the destruction of the redwood and
the loss of our natural wonder in chaotic sprawl. It counts
napalm and counts nuclear warheads and armoured cars
for the police to fight the riots in our cities. It counts
Whitman's rifle and Speck's knife, and the television
programmes which glorify violence in order to sell toys to
our children. Yet the Gross National Product does not
allow for the health of our children, the quality of their
education or the joy of their play. It does not include the
beauty of our poetry or the strength of our marriages, the
intelligence of our public debate or the integrity of our
public officials. It measures neither our wit nor our
courage, neither our wisdom nor our learning, neither our
compassion nor our devotion to our country, it measures
everything in short, except that which makes life
worthwhile. And it can tell us everything about America
except why we are proud that we are Americans.'

Robert F. Kennedy

That's a pretty damning quote from Robert Kennedy. He had a point, didn't he?

No.

You're in a combative mood.

All right, I'll qualify that. Kennedy was right, of course, that lots of important things are not included in the economic statistics that underlie the growth figures you see in the headlines. What annoys me is the suggestion that all economists care about is these figures.

We touched on this in Chapter 1.

We did, and I gave a short answer – if we care about things like inequality and the environment and happiness, then growing the economy is not a bad way to give us the means of tackling those. But I want to give a more comprehensive answer, because the critique of economics exemplified by Bobby Kennedy is one you hear a lot these days. You will often hear people criticise economics for its fixation on growth. Actually, these arguments come in two distinct flavours, which are often conflated but which it's useful to tease apart and address separately.

Argument number one goes something like this: *It's a bad idea to care about economic growth because growth is measured in*

GDP, and GDP is a flawed way of measuring. We should measure something more useful instead – something like happiness, perhaps.

Argument number two goes like this: *It's a bad idea to care about economic growth because we will ultimately hit limits in how far an economy can grow. We're going to need to live without growth eventually, so we should start learning to do so now.*

Let me spend this chapter and the next addressing the first concern, and the one after that addressing the second.

Fair enough. Let's clear up some terminology first, though. Why is Robert Kennedy talking about GNP, not GDP? What's the difference?

GDP stands for 'gross domestic product', GNP stands for 'gross national product', and a third set of initials, GNI – which refers to much the same thing as GNP but is a more descriptive name – stands for 'gross national income'. They are closely related. All of these measures are trying to add up the value of income, spending or production in a country as a whole. I say 'income, spending or production' because there are three different ways to calculate GDP and they should all, in principle, give you the same number. You can add up everybody's income – that is, salaries plus the income people earn because they own property or shares or corporate bonds. Or you can add up all the money that people spend. Or you can add up the market value of everything that everybody produces. And because one person's spending is another person's income, and because the market value of production is judged by what people spend buying it, these concepts are two sides of the same coin. Well, three sides of the same coin, but you can see what I'm trying to say.

Where the concepts differ is how you define 'in a country'. For example, if a Canadian owns a flat in London and rents it out for money, should that economic value be recorded in Canada or the United Kingdom? A similar question would occur if a Canadian company owned a factory in the United Kingdom. The answer is that a Canadian-owned asset in the United Kingdom is adding to UK GDP but to Canadian GNP or GNI. 'Gross domestic product' is the market value produced inside a country's borders, but 'gross national income' (or 'gross national product') is the income accruing to a country's citizens. If all citizens only owned assets in their home countries then GDP and GNI would be trying to measure the same thing. As it is, in some countries with very open economies – Ireland is a good example – GDP is substantially different from GNI. Irish GDP is high because lots of foreign-owned companies have set up shop there; GNI in Ireland is not so high because the Irish don't own as many investments overseas. And we usually say 'GNI' rather than 'GNP' because if you're talking about who owns an asset, you are presumably more interested in how much income it generates rather than how productive it is, albeit that the two concepts are supposed to be interchangeable.

Another difference between GDP and GNI comes when you convert them into a common currency (usually dollars) for the same purpose of making international comparisons. GDP is usually converted using prevailing foreign exchange rates, which reflect the market value of a country's exports. GNI tends to be converted at what's called 'purchasing power parity', which adjusts for living costs. For instance, if you compare the GDP per capita of Switzerland to that of the United States, you'll see that the Swiss are a good 60 per cent more productive: thanks to Zurich's banking sector and a long history of precision manufacturing, Switzerland has one of the world's highest GDPs per person. But if you look instead at GNI per person converted at purchasing power parity, you find that the US and Switzerland are pretty much on a par: the US may produce less per citizen as measured by the foreign exchange markets, but measured by what you can buy domestically with your cash, it's almost as prosperous as Switzerland because in the US it's cheaper to buy fuel, food and housing.

Right, then. Let's turn to Kennedy's point. What about the omissions? What's left out of the GDP statistics?

There's no end to the list of things that GDP doesn't measure: happiness, of course; children's playtime and stable marriages, as we've heard; health and life expectancy; inequality; human rights; corruption; carbon dioxide emissions; the time wasted in traffic jams. I could continue, but I think it's more helpful to try to focus on the things that conceptually could be included in GDP measures, but aren't.

Remember that GDP is a measure of value added in a given year, worked out using market prices as a yardstick. Given that framework, it makes sense to ask what value is added or lost and yet not recorded in the GDP statistics.

There are things that are just imponderable. As it happens, our GDP statistics do measure the value of poetry: it's the money spent buying poetry books, less the cost of printing and distributing the poetry books. You might say that that's not a very good measure of the value of poetry. All I can say in response is that your time would be better spent reading and writing poetry than it would be trying to figure out a 'better' valuation.

Then there are transactions that could, in principle, take place in the market, but don't and so lack a market price. At that point we either have to ignore them or guess what they might have been. The biggest one is the value of people living in their own home. If I moved out of my house into yours, and paid you £10,000 a year as rent, and you moved into my house and paid rent to me of £10,000 a year, then a naive measure of GDP would increase by £20,000. But the actual consumption of shelter hasn't increased: we've simply turned it from a non-market transaction into a market transaction. In fact, GDP statistics do try to correct for this problem by including an estimate of the value people derive from living in their own homes.

GDP statistics also try to estimate production by governments and charities; it tends to be valued at the cost of the inputs. In other words, if the government spends £10 billion on something, the assumption is that, well, that's £10 billion of value. Maybe if people actually had to buy the government product, they'd be willing to pay a lot more, or maybe a lot less. GDP statistics wave away that inconvenient possibility.

Other forms of non-market work are just ignored completely. The classic (and alas, sexist) illustration of this was the observation that 'if a man marries his housekeeper, GDP falls' – the point being that wives were expected to do the housework without earning a wage, and so housework performed by wives isn't part of GDP calculations.

Presumably if a millionaire playboy (as played by Richard Gere) marries a heart-of-gold prostitute (as played by Julia Roberts), then GDP also falls?

Only if we're in a place where prostitution is legal. Otherwise, it makes no difference, because grey- or black-market transactions aren't included in GDP either – for the simple reason that if they're hidden from the government, government statisticians can't easily count them. That means GDP doesn't include things like illicit drugs, counterfeit products, and jobs for which tradesmen are paid cash-in-hand.

Going back to housework, the general term for these cases is 'household production', and household production does not typically appear in GDP statistics. So a child cared for by a family member doesn't add to GDP, but a child cared for by a paid childminder does. Same goes for elderly relatives cared for at home instead of in a nursing home, vegetables grown in the back garden instead of bought in a shop, repairs you do yourself instead of calling in a tradesman, and so on.

It seems daft that a society in which parents work to pay for childcare will have a higher GDP than a society in which parents look after their own kids.

It does, on the face of it. But why does it matter? It matters only if you believe that including parental childcare in GDP would change social attitudes or government policies. Do governments really set out to incentivise commercial childcare instead of stay-at-home parenting because they want to give their GDP statistics a boost? Personally, I doubt it – but if you think differently, you're free to instruct your government statisticians accordingly.

In fact, household production has long been one of the most controversial omissions from GDP. Simon Kuznets, perhaps the most influential of the creators of modern GDP accounting, was keen to include estimates of it. He thought that would make GDP a better measure of national welfare. It was an argument he lost, at least as far as official statistics are concerned, and one which has continued to surface over the years: should GDP try to measure one thing well (market production) or should it try to be more comprehensive, at the risk of measuring many things badly?[1] I think there's a pretty good case for measuring what you can measure well.

Before I decide that, I need to know what else we miss by not trying to be more comprehensive.

The value of assets is the last big omission. If King Kong knocks down the Empire State Building, and money is spent rebuilding it, GDP may well increase. (It won't *necessarily* increase: if the economy is already working at capacity then the construction work will simply draw resources away from other projects without raising economic output; the issues here are much the same as we discussed in our chapter on fiscal stimulus.) But if you had an iconic skyscraper, lost it and then spent $10 billion having to replace it, it seems odd to record the $10 billion spent as 'GDP' without mentioning the loss of a building worth $10 billion in the first place.

This issue is particularly obvious when it comes to environmental assets. If Qatar produces four trillion cubic feet of natural gas and sells the gas, GDP will record the proceeds of the sale. The fact that there are now four trillion fewer cubic feet of gas under Qatar will probably not even get a footnote, but you don't have to be a panda-hugging environmentalist to spot that something is missing from the calculation.

This sounds like a serious omission. Can't we include environmental assets in GDP?

In principle, yes. We could also value ozone depletion, the accumulation of greenhouse gases in the atmosphere, water quality, fish stocks – the list is, unfortunately, a long one. There have been attempts to produce a value for 'ecosystem services' – one, published in 1997 by a large team of researchers, reckoned that the ecosystem provided benefits worth one to three times the world's GDP, which was $18 trillion at the time.[2] That sort of estimate seems daft: it's pretty obvious that if we lacked sunlight, oxygen and water, we would all be dead. On what basis, then, does it make much sense to put a value on the world's ecosystem and tack it onto our GDP figures?

But on a more local basis there's a good case for trying to measure the value of ecosystem services that might be enhanced or destroyed by human activity. It is certainly important to try to value the ecosystem when it comes to working out the appropriate level of a carbon dioxide tax, or deciding whether to allow a developer to drain wetlands and stick an airport on top of them. Such environmental benefits can't be easy to estimate, but unless we plan to make such decisions on the basis of pure ideological prejudice, you need to try. As for adding all this to GDP? I have no strong objections, but the key question is whether such statistical efforts will help you make better decisions.

So you're saying GDP simply can't be improved as a means of measurement?

No. There are certainly specific technical fixes you could make, with the help of some trusted statisticians. One might be to include depreciation – calculating 'net domestic product' instead of GDP. Depreciation, the declining value of old assets, is hard to measure. But with the rapid obsolescence of computers and other IT equipment, it is getting hard to ignore. A second issue is the value of services as opposed to manufactured goods: services are hard to value, particularly when trying to adjust for quality – if the price of a haircut or a restaurant meal in my neighbourhood doubles over the course of a couple of years is that because of inflation or because the area is gentrifying and new fancy places have opened to offer a more refined product? This is a tricky task for the statisticians, but services are now such a large part of the economy, they, too, call out for closer statistical attention.

Here's another, particularly topical issue: valuing financial services. Andrew Haldane of the Bank of England points out that in the UK, banks made their largest ever contribution to GDP growth in the final quarter of 2008 – the quarter immediately following the collapse of Lehman Brothers and the implosion of the banking system across the world. This, quite obviously, reflects the fact that we don't do a good job of measuring the value of banking. There's a good case for poking around in such dark corners of the GDP statistics.

I still can't believe there isn't some more useful figure that I can look at instead of GDP, something more comprehensive.

Such as?

I'm sure I've read in the news about indexes of national happiness, or suchlike. Maybe I could try to get my country to the top of that.

Perhaps you're thinking of the Happy Planet Index. It was launched back in 2006 by the New Economics Foundation. They discovered that Vanuatu, a little chain of islands in the Pacific, was the happiest place on the planet. There was a lot of press coverage about Vanuatu's lovely beaches, sunshine, polygamous culture and lack of income tax. Unfortunately, not much of that press coverage reported what the actual Happy Planet Index measured. It wasn't happiness.

What did it measure, then?

It was a measure of – well, at the risk of sounding unkind, I would have to say that it was a measure of the policy agenda of the New Economics Foundation.

The Happy Planet Index took a measure of happiness, multiplied it by an estimate of life expectancy, and then divided it by a measure of the ecological footprint of the country in question. It was more of an attempt to measure environmental efficiency: if you can get long lives of bliss without damaging the natural order of things, that's a recipe for topping the Happy Planet Index. Now in the case of Vanuatu, the calculation was as follows: life expectancy of 68.6 years was multiplied by life satisfaction of 7.4 on a scale of 1–10, and the result was divided by an environmental footprint of 1.1. (The details of how that footprint was calculated don't really matter: you get the idea.)

The result was 461, presumably measured in 'bliss-years per footprint'.

The US environmental footprint was 9.5. So to reach 462 bliss-years per footprint and top the Vanuatuans, US citizens needed to rack up 4389 bliss-years each. By definition, life satisfaction can't go above 10. Therefore, to beat Vanuatu on the Happy Planet Index, and assuming that all US citizens lived lives of unadulterated orgasmic bliss from birth to death, US life expectancy would need to rise to 439 years. It's a tall order.[3]

The other way for the US to rise to the top of the Happy Planet Index, of course, would be dramatically to reduce its ecological footprint. Which is all very well, but it might have been better for the New Economics Foundation just to call for us to consume fewer material resources. Instead the NEF produced the Happy Planet Index as a roundabout way of getting press coverage for the idea. Since many of the newspapers lazily mistook it for a raw measure of happiness, I am not even sure the idea worked on its own terms.

And, actually, it gets worse. The New Economics Foundation didn't even ask the Vanuatuans how happy they were. Nobody did. The place is too small, with a population less than a tenth that of the New York borough of Brooklyn. The happiness number that went into the Happy Planet Index in 2006 was an estimate based on how happy other, apparently comparable countries are. The whole episode isn't that pretty: a ranking was constructed to publicise the priorities of a particular think tank, the media lapped it up without reading the small print (or indeed, most of the large print), and the country that made the headlines should never have been included in the ranking at all because the relevant data didn't exist.

OK. Perhaps I shouldn't gear my policy towards climbing up the Happy Planet Index.

To be fair, it's not just the New Economics Foundation. All kinds of organisations have discovered that if you publish some kind of ranking you can get cheap media attention. The pro-market Heritage Institute publishes the Index of Economic Freedom, with Hong Kong on top; the United Nations Development Programme (UNDP) publishes the Human Development Index, which lauds Norway; and Transparency International publishes the Perceptions of

Corruption Index, with Denmark top and Somalia and Afghanistan at the bottom.

Now, the New Economics Foundation wants to promote a happy planet, the Heritage Institute is in favour of economic freedom, the UNDP wants human development, and Transparency International battles corruption. But just because government statistical offices compile data on GDP growth, that doesn't mean that all governments care about is GDP growth.

You've made the case against the Happy Planet Index. You haven't made the case for using rankings based on GDP instead.

Nor would I want to. If governments published a ranking of GDP per capita, as these think tanks do to get their media coverage, then the country at the top of the list would probably be Qatar or Luxembourg or Liechtenstein or Monaco or Bermuda. None of them has important economic lessons to teach us about running an economy. The Heritage Institute argues that Hong Kong is a model, the UNDP says the same about Norway – but I really don't see what lesson we could learn from Qatar or Bermuda. Clearly anyone can make a ranking based on GNI or GDP per capita – there are several on Wikipedia – but I don't think such rankings have any great influence on government policy. Which brings us to the core of the problem with attacks on GDP like Robert Kennedy's. They rely on the popular misconception that GDP is some kind of fetish; that much of what is wrong with the way the economy is organised is wrong because we collect GDP stat-istics, and that the way to fix our economic problems is to measure something else. I think that's just a mistake. Robert Kennedy's speech is beautiful and powerful, but it also includes a rhetorical bait-and-switch. He begins by saying, 'we seemed to have surrendered personal excellence and community values in the mere accumulation of material things', and per-haps that is true. A moment later, he is pointing out that GNP doesn't measure the joy as children play, the value of a strong marriage or the beauty of poetry. Well, indeed.

But if you actually rephrase the rhetoric as a logical argu-ment, it begins to look a bit suspicious: 'We have surrendered personal excellence and community values. We no longer read good poetry, nor do we allow our children to play as much as we once did, and divorce rates are on the increase. And why is this? It's because government statistical offices have sprung up almost from nowhere since the early 1930s, gathering esti-mates of the productive potential of the economy. It is clear that by gathering and publishing these statistics, they have undermined our appreciation for art, our commitment to traditional ideals of marriage, and our qualities as parents.' Come again? Is that really how it happened?

But we talk about GDP all the time! How can you suggest it's not the aim of government policy?

I'm not saying it's completely irrelevant to government policy, of course. I just don't think it's anywhere near being the bogeyman that some of its critics seem to think.

For starters, don't forget that economic growth happens whether or not we're trying to measure it. At the end of the nineteenth century, Europe and the United States experienced an economic transformation unprecedented in human history. This burst of incredible economic growth was based on many of the things that make critics of GDP uneasy: the industrialisation of farming; the exploitation of the most carbon-intensive of all fossil fuels, coal; and massive movement of workers from the countryside into the cities and their dangerous, smoky factories. But all this happened before GDP was a twinkle in a statistician's eye. The economists of the time could see it happening – everybody could – but they couldn't measure it. Economic growth didn't suddenly start to happen when government statisticians started measuring GDP.

Nonetheless, modern politicians know that GDP growth figures have an impact on their popularity.

And so do many other things. Do you really believe government ministers wake up in the morning and think, 'What can I do to increase GDP?' In the month I am writing this paragraph, British government ministers or officials were discussing the following economic policies: whether or not to leave the European Union (a decision that had nothing to do with GDP); launching a revised pension system (designed to simplify the system and mildly redistribute, again nothing to do with GDP); deciding not to fix a flaw in the way inflation was calculated (a decision with redistributive consequences but irrelevant to

GDP); and various education reforms (designed to improve educational outcomes, again with no reference to GDP).

Politicians realise that even within the narrow economic realm, people have other priorities – fairness, concern over rising prices, the quality of public services, freedom, fear of unemployment – that are at best merely correlated with GDP, and at worst have nothing to do with it. Successful ministers will focus on those problems, not on some abstract statistical construct.

Why collect statistics at all, then?

Statistics are useful when they help you make better policy decisions. This generally does not include the kind of rankings churned out by think tanks attempting to promote a particular idea of the good life. Such public relations exercises tell you very little that you can actually turn into action.

And don't forget that a lot of the most useful data your government statisticians can collect isn't to do with the economy as a whole. You may be concerned about domestic violence, perhaps, or species extinction, or childhood literacy. If so, measure the problem as best you can and commission good-quality research, such as randomised policy trials, to help develop a solution. Of course, conceptually, you could try to put a monetary value on the 'psychic cost' of domestic violence, and you could subtract that value from GDP. But it probably isn't the best way to deal with the problem. And just because you don't account for domestic violence in GDP figures, doesn't mean you don't care about domestic violence.

Anyway, why feel that you have to produce a single number that summarises everything? All aggregates are statistical compromises: inflation statistics measure the price of a 'typical' basket of goods, which will not reflect your individual shopping habits, or mine; in compiling employment numbers you will have to find some way of acknowledging part-time work. Some degree of aggregation is inevitable, but do also remember that you can measure inflation, inequality, unemployment and GDP without having to produce some amorphous summary of all four of them. All of these measures, and others, are useful in informing your policy priorities. None should monopolise your attention.

Still, though, if I care about my people being happy, can't I also measure their happiness directly and consider this in my policymaking, too?

Yes, if you like. Let's talk about that in a new chapter.

12

Happynomics

'Politicians mistakenly believe that economic growth makes a nation happier ... But today there is much statistical and laboratory evidence in favour of a heresy: once a country has filled its larders there is no point in that nation becoming richer. The hippies, the Greens, the road protesters, the down-shifters, the slow-food movement – all are having their quiet revenge. Routinely derided, the ideas of these down-to-earth philosophers are being confirmed by new statistical work by psychologists and economists.'

Professor Andrew Oswald, 'The Hippies Were Right All along about Happiness', *Financial Times*, 19 January 2006

Andrew Oswald is a clever man. I told you that we should be measuring happiness.

I never said that you shouldn't; I just mused that it might not help you make better decisions. As a matter of fact, many countries already do gather official data on happiness. It's not much trouble to do so – just a few more questions on a survey that was going to be conducted anyway. And in many of the countries that don't gather this data, Gallup, a private polling company, does. David Cameron became British Prime Minister promising to commission new measures of well-being; the then President of France, Nicolas Sarkozy, had already done the same. Barack Obama appointed a number of leading happiness researchers, including Betsey Stevenson, Alan Krueger and Cass Sunstein, to senior government positions. The remote mountain kingdom of Bhutan has been talking about 'gross national happiness' for many years. So if you're serious about this happynomics thing, all I can say is that you're joining the in-crowd.[1]

But you're sceptical.

Yes and no. I think it's a good idea to collect this kind of data but I think that it's being oversold, for a variety of reasons. But why don't we run through how happiness is measured and what we've learned so far, and you can judge for yourself?

Broadly speaking there are three ways to measure a country's well-being. The first is to take national accounts and tweak them to reflect the cost of resource depletion, traffic jams, unpaid labour and so on. This is the approach Simon Kuznets favoured and we've discussed it quite fully already. A second way is to pull together a grab-bag of relevant data, anything from life expectancy to the murder rate, income inequality to the prevalence of depression. Most civilised countries will have such data already, but it varies in quality.

But the third way is to go out and ask people how they feel – that is, to try to directly measure happiness (or as economists and psychologists in the field tend to call it, 'subjective well-being'). The most popular way to do that is also the simplest: ask people how satisfied they are with their lives. The staple question about overall life satisfaction, as lovingly spoofed by the journalist and statistical guru Michael Blastland, is this: 'When all's said and done, at the end of the day Brian, taking the rough with the smooth and all that, rate your well-being on a scale of one to 10.'[2]

They really ask that?

Of course they don't ask exactly that. But Mr Blastland has given you the gist of it. Originally it was common to simply ask, 'Taken as a whole, how happy would you say you are these days? Very happy, fairly happy, or not very happy.' Score that result on a scale of 1–3 and you can tot up how happy everyone is.

While the question says 'taken as a whole ...' people find it difficult to do that. Our subjective assessments of how satisfied we are with our entire lives can be influenced by something as ephemeral as a sunny day. The University of Michigan psychologist Norbert Schwarz demonstrated the effect of apparently trivial context with a rather splendid experiment. He asked people in an office environment to complete a life satisfaction survey, but asked them to make a photocopy of the survey before they did. For half of the subjects, the cunning Professor Schwarz had left a dime on the copier glass where, of course, they would find it. It turns out that finding a dime just before you fill in a happiness survey makes you more satisfied with your life as a whole.

The economist Angus Deaton has found that people's happiness during the darkest days of the crisis, 2008–10, was closely correlated with what the stock market was doing. That may be because both happiness and the stock market were being driven by some third factor (perhaps by a clear-eyed view of the future prospects for the economy; perhaps by the weather). Another explanation, which I find plausible, is that people watch the stock prices on the morning news and their mood is influenced for the day.[3]

Whatever their limitations, these surveys are the foundation of most studies of happiness and the most influential paper in happiness economics, Richard Easterlin's 1974 'Does Economic Growth Improve the Human Lot?', extensively discusses evidence from them.[4]

Very few American respondents said that they were 'not very happy'. Almost half said they were 'very happy', the most blissful response available. Americans, then, are generally happy with life – too happy, perhaps, for a three-point scale. A great deal has been made of the observation that Americans have not become much happier since the 1950s, although they are now much richer. But if half of all Americans already said they were 'very happy' in the 1950s and the average response was around 2.5 on a scale of 1–3, how much happier could we have expected them to become? Easterlin is often quoted as having proved that economic growth does not lead to happiness, but perhaps we should instead say he found evidence that economic growth does not eliminate misery.

These days the scale often ranges from 1 to 7, or sometimes 0 to 10, which clearly gives more scope for variation – although the scope is hardly unlimited. The United States can be (and is) a hundred times richer than, say, Liberia, but on a scale of 1 to 3 or 1 to 7 it simply cannot be a hundred times happier. That is a simple fact about the way we measure these things that is often swept under the carpet.

And this Richard Easterlin fellow is responsible for the idea that money doesn't buy happiness?

I think that Buddhism is responsible for the idea that money doesn't buy happiness. Richard Easterlin actually discovered something rather more subtle and puzzling, which is why his finding is usually called the 'Easterlin paradox'.

Easterlin discovered that money very much does buy happiness – within the context of a given society. Richer people tend to be happier than poorer people. This is an extremely robust result, although it's worth pointing out that other things – divorce, unemployment, ill-health – have a far larger impact on happiness than mere lack of cash does.

Easterlin's paradox is as follows: while richer people are happier than poorer people, richer societies are not happier than poorer societies. To put it another way, getting a pay rise of 10 per cent will make you happier. But economic growth of 10 per cent will not make the society around you happier.

I can see why they call it a paradox. What's the explanation?

There are three possible explanations.

One possibility is that these questions just don't tell us much over time. I mean, if I ask a Portuguese trawlerman in 1955 how happy he is on a scale of 1–3 (in Portuguese), and I also ask a Japanese salaryman the same question in the 1970s (in Japanese), and then a German housewife the same question in the 1990s (in German) – do I really learn anything by comparing the answers? It's reasonable to compare people within the same society, using the same language, at the same time – but it's certainly open to doubt that we can learn anything comparing different societies across time.

That original Easterlin paper, for instance, contains this intriguing nugget, based on a 1965 survey: 53 per cent of the British respondents were 'very happy' but only 20 per cent of West Germans and 12 per cent of the French. Income per head was similar at the time. More recently a Eurobarometer survey found that 64 per cent of Danes described themselves as 'very satisfied' while only 16 per cent of French people did. Should we really conclude that the French are unhappy? Should we conclude anything much at all? Linguists caution that it's lazy and unjustifiable to assume that other languages even have a precise analogy for 'happy'.[5]

And as a thought experiment, imagine that instead of calculating GDP, we measured economic growth by asking people in a survey, 'How rich would you say you are these days? Very rich, fairly rich or not at all rich?' Think about the quality of data that might result, and how it might change over time. And imagine I said I was 'fairly rich', but had never heard of Bill Gates. Then I watched a documentary about Bill Gates and revised my answer to 'not at all rich'. It wouldn't mean I had less money, or even that I felt poorer – simply that I had revised my views about what sort of wealth was possible. Perhaps it's the same with happiness: perhaps we feel happier than our parents were but have subconsciously adjusted our ideas about how happy one might reasonably expect to feel. Or perhaps not; it's hard to know.

A second possibility is that these international surveys do tell us something but that, because Easterlin had to use the sketchy data that was available in the 1970s, his conclusions no longer stand up. For example, Japan's average happiness seemed to stagnate even while its economy was booming. But as the questionnaires from Japan have been re-translated, it has become clear that the reason people seemed less satisfied was that the questions kept changing, raising the bar for happiness.

A number of economists, including Betsey Stevenson, have published research arguing that when happiness is properly measured, money buys happiness *for* a society in exactly the same way that money buys happiness *within* a society. Stevenson's co-author Justin Wolfers told me that the relationship between life satisfaction and income is 'one of the highest correlations you'll ever see in a cross-country data set in the social sciences, ever'.[6]

But Easterlin and others have fought back with their own analysis. My conclusion: the jury is out. The Easterlin paradox may not exist at all, but it's too early to write it off.

The third explanation for the Easterlin paradox is to take it at face value and conclude that what people care about isn't absolute income, but relative income – their economic position within society. Another way of interpreting it is that what really makes people happy is not so much income but status – a zero-sum game in the sense that if you climb up the pecking order, someone else has to slip down – and that status is strongly correlated with income. So perhaps money doesn't buy happiness, but *being richer than other people* does.

This third hypothesis does sound awfully plausible.

There is a famous survey by the economists Sara Solnick and David Hemenway often summarised thus: if you ask people whether they'd rather have an income of $50,000 in a world where everyone else had $25,000, or an income of $100,000 in a world where everyone else had $200,000, you'll find that people prefer the former option – that is, they'd rather be relatively rich than absolutely rich.[7] You should take this with a grain of salt: most of Solnick and Hemenway's respondents were students at Harvard University, who may be a particularly competitive bunch. When the researchers asked Harvard *staff*, only a third of them agreed.

Still, the idea that people care mostly about their income relative to their peer group is so enormously plausible that, despite all the difficulties with the data, it would take a great deal to convince people that Richard Easterlin is wrong.

I certainly find Easterlin's conclusion persuasive. And this just shows that we should devote more resources to measuring happiness properly. I don't want to leave Bhutan being the only country in the world to value 'gross national happiness'.

Ah, yes – Bhutan. The Himalayan mountain kingdom provides the clearest example I can think of that there's a difference between collecting statistics about happiness, and making people happy. Bhutan is venerated by the more naive happiness wonks . . .

How rude.

... As I was saying, Bhutan is venerated by the more naive happiness wonks, who seem unaware of its rather dubious human rights record. According to Human Rights Watch, many members of Bhutan's Nepali minority have been stripped of their citizenship and harassed out of the country. Although of course if they were miserable to start with, that kind of ethnic cleansing might indeed raise average happiness levels – in Bhutan itself, if not in refugee camps across the border in Nepal.[8]

Funnily enough the 'gross national happiness' thing appears to have emerged as a defensive reflex – the then King of Bhutan, Jigme Singye Wangchuck, announced that 'Gross National Happiness is more important than Gross Domestic Product' when pressed on the question of Bhutan's lack of economic progress in an interview with the *Financial Times* in 1986. His Majesty isn't the last person to turn to alternative measures of progress for consolation. When Nicolas Sarkozy was President of France he commissioned Professors Stiglitz, Sen and Fitoussi to contemplate alternatives to GDP; one possible reason for President Sarkozy's enthusiasm was surely that the French spend most of their time not working, and this lowers France's GDP. The country is likely to look better on most alternative indices. It's not unreasonable to look at those alternatives, but let's not kid ourselves: politicians are always on the lookout for statistical measures that reflect well on them.

You mentioned that President Obama had appointed several happynomics experts. Same story there?

Less so, perhaps, because none of the appointees – Alan Krueger, Betsey Stevenson and Cass Sunstein – had day jobs that focused on happiness economics. But Professor Krueger has been doing some very interesting work on subjective well-being with the psychologists Norbert Schwartz and Daniel Kahneman – Kahneman being the Nobel laureate whose work we've already encountered in the context of sticky prices.[9]

Kahneman points out that 'happiness' is a fuzzy concept. 'The concept of happiness has to be reorganised,' he told me in an interview in the autumn of 2010. There are really three concepts here: there's the kind of subjective summary measured in Easterlin's work (and most other happiness economics), where we ask people how satisfied they are with their lives; then there is the sort of ongoing emotional stream – first tired, then laughing, then stressed, then joyful, then aroused – that we might argue adds up to an enjoyable life (or not); and then there is some external effort to measure somebody's welfare against objective criteria (are they having trouble sleeping, do they have health problems, etc., etc.). A lot of lazy thinking puts all three together and calls them 'happiness'. But they are not the same – and happiness itself, a wonderfully flexible term, arguably means something more than any of these things.

Kahneman and his colleagues are trying to measure the stream of emotional states – or more specifically, to track the amount of time in a day that a person spends feeling some kind of negative emotion such as fear, anger or sadness. The 'day reconstruction method' asks people to recall, episode by episode, the previous day's events and the most prevalent accompanying feeling – enthusiasm, boredom, joy, irritation.

Kahneman, incidentally, published a paper with Angus Deaton that throws light on the question of money and happiness.[10] Kahneman and Deaton found that higher income is correlated with life satisfaction, without limit – but beyond an income of about $75,000 a year, extra money does not improve your mood as measured by day reconstruction.

So whether or not money buys happiness depends on what you mean by happiness.

Quite so. Day reconstruction produces quite different results from the more traditional surveys of life satisfaction. One survey comparing women in France to those in Ohio found that the American women were twice as likely to say they were very satisfied with their lives. And yet it was the French women who spent more of their day in a good mood. Enjoyment as experienced minute by minute is not the same as a once-and-for-all judgement about how satisfying life is.

If you really plan not only to measure happiness but to use it to influence policy, this is a distinction you will have to start taking seriously.

Does it have different implications for policy?

Well, that's a very good question.

If you believe Richard Easterlin's explanation of his paradox – that people don't care about absolute income, only about income relative to others – then that would obviously be an argument for redistributive taxation. After all, by taking money from the rich you make everyone else happier, even before you've spent the cash. Yet of course we already have redistributive taxation; whether we should have *more* redistribution than we already do is not so clear. Another policy implication from life satisfaction research is that you should try very hard to reduce unemployment because it is such an extremely depressing experience – although I would hope that this would be on your agenda already.

Another possibility is to use life satisfaction data to work out appropriate damages for people who have been injured or bereaved. British economist Andrew Oswald has data on how such misfortunes make people feel, along with how much money might be expected to offset the emotional impact of such traumatic events. But while this may be a useful practice, it is hardly the stuff of macroeconomic policy.

You're making it sound like this is all pointless.

It's not pointless; it's just not revolutionary either. Remember that many countries already collect data on life satisfaction, and it's not much trouble to collect a bit more; it's simply a case of adding more questions to pre-existing surveys.

The day reconstruction method used by Professors Kahneman and Krueger is more costly to collect but might also be more useful for informing policy. Kahneman and

Krueger have been advocating the publication of 'time accounting' measures alongside regular national accounts. These time accounts are being tacked on to a well-established part of the US statistical apparatus, the time-use survey, which asks people how they're spending their time – commuting, praying, watching television or having lunch. The innovation is to combine these time-use surveys with the day reconstruction method to produce a measure of how much of their day people spend in an unpleasant mood, along with a record of what they are doing while they experience that mood.

I'm curious . . .

OK. Commuting and working are the activities most likely to induce a bad mood. Lunch, dinner and having sex are rarely regarded as unpleasant, although if you pick the wrong spouse then all three can presumably be pretty disappointing.

You're saying I should ban work and subsidise sex?

Wouldn't that be nice? But seriously, you can see how these national time accounts could help evaluate projects such as investments which reduce commuting time (new roads or high-speed rail), or provide amenities such as parks, playgrounds and museums. Of course, we cannot fully escape the problem of comparing my six-out-of-ten to your five-out-of-ten – but the day reconstruction method, measuring how much time we each spend engaged in activities that turn our moods sour, may prove slightly more objective.

The Kahneman–Krueger team has developed a stripped-down version of the day reconstruction method, which can be conducted as a regular telephone survey, and the Bureau of Labor Statistics has already conducted its first survey with the new method. We'll see what emerges – perhaps you can use the technique yourself.

Perhaps. Well, thanks for talking it through with me.

My pleasure.

Happy now?

13

Can growth continue for ever?

'What can we reasonably expect the level of our economic life to be a hundred years hence? What are the economic possibilities for our grandchildren?'

John Maynard Keynes, 'Economic Possibilities for our Grandchildren', March 1930

You wanted this chapter to be about the limits to growth, right?

Right. Pretty much everything I've said so far has been predicated on the assumption that economic growth is a good thing. This bothers some people. Especially physicists, it seems.

Funny you should mention that. Since I've been put in charge of the economy, people have been sending me links to YouTube videos featuring physicists talking about exponential growth.

People keep sending me the links, too. There's physicist Albert

Bartlett's 'The Most Important Video You'll Ever See' – I'm going to be kind and assume Professor Bartlett didn't choose his own title – which has racked up five million views or so, despite being a film of a static lecture by an elderly chap to a small classroom with the key message, 'the greatest short-coming of the human race is our inability to understand the exponential function'. A more recent and very popular riff on a similar topic comes in the shape of a blog post entitled 'Exponential Economist Meets Finite Physicist' by Tom Murphy, another physicist.[1]

What do they say?

The key issue is that exponential growth will eventually take you to impossible places. And by 'eventually', they mean 'sooner than we expect'.

Exponential growth is any kind of growth that compounds like interest payments. The classic example is the rice on the chessboard. According to an old story, the inventor of the game of chess was offered a reward by a delighted king. He requested a modest-sounding payment: one grain of rice on the first square of the chessboard, two on the second, four on the third, doubling each time. Intuitively one imagines that, with only sixty-four squares on a chessboard, the whole thing will add up to a few sacks of rice at most. It's actually a colossal amount – many times the annual rice production of the entire planet. This is Professor Bartlett's point: we simply struggle to wrap our minds around the implications of exponential growth.

The chessboard prize was 100 per cent growth per square; but 10 per cent, 1 per cent or even 0.0001 per cent – it's all exponential growth. And it all becomes trouble eventually, because each little bit of growth will itself be multiplied by growth in the future. As Albert Einstein, yet another physicist, is famously said to have declared (but probably did not), 'The most powerful force in the universe is compound interest.'

The implication for economic growth seems obvious. Our economy grows at a few per cent a year. That hasn't presented many insuperable problems so far. But exponential growth is exponential growth, and eventually – the physicists worry – we'll reach a square on the economic chessboard that we just can't fill.

That sounds like an argument that strikes at the very heart of economics.

On the contrary, economists understand this point perfectly well. One of the very first people to be called an economist was the Reverend Thomas Malthus, who died almost two hundred years ago. Malthus's reputation is built on 'An Essay on the Principle of Population', in which he explained that trouble was in store because human population grows exponentially and so eventually will become unsustainable. It doesn't matter how quickly, say, agricultural productivity grows. If that growth is arithmetical – 10, 20, 30, 40, 50 – then it will inevitably be overtaken by the exponential progress of human population growth – 2, 4, 8, 16, 32, 64.

And that will be true regardless of what the population growth rate actually is, as long as it's more than zero, and proportional to the existing population. So this is hardly a problem that's failed to occur to the economic profession.

Interesting to see you embracing Malthus. I thought that economists had been ridiculing him for most of the last two centuries.

I have to admit that's largely true. Malthus's timing was unfortunate. He explained that human population would be held in check by the availability of food; we might not starve to death, but we could certainly expect that every time some technological advance raised living standards, population growth would eventually eat up the slack and bring living standards crashing down again to subsistence levels. And he was wrong. The maths is incontrovertible but the assumptions were flawed: technological progress was faster than population growth in the short term, and more recently population growth has been slowing down dramatically. There's every reason to believe that the population of the planet is going to stabilise.

And zero population growth – well, I am not sure why that is supposed to be unsustainable.

GDP growth will continue, though, even if population growth stabilises. Won't that eventually fall foul of the rice-on-the-chessboard problem?

I think that here we find a serious gap in the logic of the exponential doomsayers. They're looking at exponential growth in *physical* processes – things like heating, cooling, lighting, movement. This is understandable, because they are, after all, physicists. Tom Murphy's blog post is particularly startling on this point. He points out that if our energy consumption grows at 2.3 per cent a year – less than historical rates but enough to increase energy consumption tenfold each century – then the entire planet will reach boiling point in just four centuries. It's not the greenhouse effect at work; it's irrelevant to Professor Murphy's point whether the energy comes from fossil fuels, solar power or fairy dust. This is simply about the waste heat given off, inevitably, when we use energy to do useful work. And it's pretty hard to argue with the laws of thermodynamics. The calculation sounds shocking, but it's just the rice on the chessboard all over again.

Here's the logic lapse: energy growth is not the same as economic growth. GDP merely measures what people are willing to pay for, which is not necessarily connected to the use of energy, or any other physical resource. True, since the beginning of the industrial revolution the two have tended to go hand in hand, but there's no logical reason why that tendency needs to continue. Indeed, it appears to have stopped already. Would you like to take a guess at energy growth per person in the United States over the last quarter of a century?

Less than 2.3 per cent, I expect you are about to say.

Not just less than 2.3 per cent. Less than zero. I compared 1986 with 2011 and got a rate of minus 0.17 per cent. Economic growth per person in the same period averaged more than 2.5 per cent. Over twenty-five years, GDP as a whole almost doubled, but energy use rose by less than a quarter. If I had picked a different time period then I would have got a slightly different number, but the story would have been the same: energy use per person isn't increasing in the United States. It peaked back in 1978. (Admittedly, some of this energy consumption is 'offshored' in the form of manufacturing in China or Mexico which is then imported. But the offshoring effect just doesn't seem that big: imports comprise less than 20 per cent of the US economy, and of course we have to offset imported energy consumption against all the things the US makes domestically but exports abroad.)

It's the same picture for Japan, the UK and the European Union – all of which, I might mention, have far lower energy use per person than the United States. The very highest energy consumption per person in the history of the UK was in 1973; in Germany it was 1979. In Japan the peak was more recent – the year 2000. But the general picture in all of these countries is the same: the economies have grown but energy consumption per person has been flat, or even somewhat declined. In the UK, energy consumption per person is at its lowest point for fifty years. Forecasting is a hazardous business, but with energy consumption per person falling in rich countries, and population growth slowing dramatically, there is no reason why energy consumption should continue to rise indefinitely.

It's easy to grasp why exponential economic growth is not the same as exponential energy growth. If I'm worried about money I may turn off my heating and wear a coat and hat indoors; a bit of extra money will mean I take off the hat and coat and use more energy. But that doesn't mean that if I win the lottery I will celebrate by boiling myself alive.

Likewise, I like food but there's only so much I can eat, and while I am sure that some fancy cuisine involves more waste, I can't imagine the amount of food I spoil increasing exponentially. The clothes of the rich and famous don't weigh any more than the clothes that you or I wear.

The rich will waste more, though – wearing clothes once and then simply throwing them away.

True enough. But a lot of what's going on with GDP growth is not that more materials are being used, but rather that much the same materials become more valuable as they are used in a better-designed object. This is true of food and clothes, my computer, my bicycle, my washing machine. We probably could burn a lot of energy in a hurry if we all started using flying cars, jetpacks or teleporters, but I am not going to lose sleep over the possibility right now.

Look, I fully agree with the environmentalists who worry that we cannot continue consuming more and more water, spewing out more and more carbon dioxide, and burning more and more coal. The problem comes if we then leap to the conclusion that the economy itself cannot keep growing. It doesn't follow. The economy has been dematerialising:

more and more of what we consume in rich countries requires fewer resources because of more efficient technology (LEDs instead of incandescent bulbs; laptops instead of mainframe computers), or because the value is mostly in the aesthetic design (haute couture, haute cuisine), or even because – like the eBook you may be reading or the audiobook you downloaded – the product is digital and has almost no physical form at all.

Think of New York City. It's a high-income place, and has for over a century been a creative powerhouse: publishing, music, fashion, art, finance, software, you name it. But energy consumption per person in New York City is lower than in the US as a whole – in fact, it's lower than the average in any American state. Ultimately, we can do a lot of the things we value – including value in the grubby pecuniary sense of 'are willing to pay lots of cash for' – without expending vast amounts of energy.

Maybe in the future we'll all end up simply being uploaded into virtual reality machines, where we can experience any and every delight imaginable. We do, after all, spend rather a lot of time enjoying ourselves in virtual spaces from Facebook to World of Warcraft. Perhaps future economic growth will revolve around longevity, freedom from discomfort, and other medical advances. Perhaps we will have kitchen-top machines that will take unwanted material and transform it into some gorgeous new toy. Nobody knows. The point is that economic growth and energy growth are not the same thing, and there are good reasons to believe they're already in the process of decoupling from each other.

Forgive me if I find it hard to imagine exponential economic growth among brains floating in virtual reality vats. Let's just imagine that economic growth is more connected to physical resources than you think, and that there comes a point where we have to accept zero economic growth. Doesn't that undermine the whole way we think about economics?

I don't think that deep down our economic model really does depend on growth, but the question is worth examining. Here's the problem: technological progress means we produce more and more economic output per hour; unless we keep growing the economy for ever, one of two things must eventually happen. Either we all learn to work less hard, perhaps working two-day weeks and enjoying five-day weekends of robots fetching us coffee and giving us back-rubs. Or we get mass unemployment.

On the evidence so far, we don't seem to be terribly good at converting wealth into leisure. Keynes famously wondered about this problem in a 1930 essay called 'Economic Possibilities for our Grandchildren'. He reckoned that – all being well – we would have met all our basic material needs by 2030, and our 'real ... permanent problem' would be how to use our freedom from material concerns; how to occupy our leisure hours 'to live wisely and agreeably and well'. As we close in on 2030, we find Keynes was pretty much spot on as far as economic growth was concerned. But the problem of filling our endless hours of leisure hasn't yet risen to the top of the agenda. We still work hard, if not quite as hard as we once did. Time-use surveys show that between 1965 and 2003, American women acquired about 4–6 hours a week of extra leisure time, and American men did even better, gaining

6–8 hours a week.[2] We also live longer, spend more time in school and university, and retire earlier than we used to – so the percentage of our lives that we spend working is on the way down. But it's falling far more slowly than Keynes expected, given the growth in GDP.

Doesn't that therefore suggest that if economic growth stops, but growth in output per hour worked keeps rising because of technological progress, some people will work flat out, while most will be jobless?

Well, perhaps – if we continue to act as we do today. One possible response – advocated by the economist Robert Frank – is to tax consumption. The more you consume, the more you pay. As the tax on consumption rises, it becomes more and more attractive to take time off and go for a stroll, or paint a watercolour. We already do something quite like this in most advanced economies, with progressive income taxes. (A consumption tax is like an income tax with an exemption for any money that you save or invest instead of spending.) But perhaps we should do more. You're in charge – see how the fancy takes you.

But isn't there another reason that our economy is hooked on growth? Don't we need growth to be able to pay off our debts?

That's not quite true. Increasing income does make debts easier to bear. Your mortgage is going to be easier to repay if you get a pay rise every year than if your income stays the same until you retire. But that doesn't mean it's impossible to repay your mortgage if you never get a pay rise. Likewise, all a zero-growth economy would mean is that each generation would be no richer than the generation before it. Even without increasing future incomes to look forward to, people would still have good reason to run up debt. You might still borrow money to go to college, to buy your first car, and to buy a house. You would pay off those debts and start saving for a pension. Eventually you'd retire and live off your savings. Just because economic growth has stopped doesn't mean that people wouldn't want to move their purchasing power around using debt.

I agree that in a zero-growth world, governments would have to rethink some things. They wouldn't be able to base the funding of their pension and healthcare benefit systems on the hope that each generation would be larger and richer than the previous one, and could comfortably pick up the bill. Nor could they routinely run small deficits in the knowledge that the debt burden would stay stable as a proportion of GDP. Governments might even find it sensible to pay off all their debts gradually – even accumulate assets, as a few resource-rich countries already do. In the long run, in a low- or zero-growth economic system, everyone from individuals to governments would have to be more careful about debts than they have been in recent years. Some may see that as revolutionary; I'd consider it a modest change in behaviour.

No need for me to click on those YouTube links, then?

I would suggest focusing on the real problem. If you are concerned about carbon dioxide emissions – and I think you should be – then find a way to raise the cost of emitting carbon dioxide. A carbon tax could do the job; so could an emission permit scheme. Ditto for energy use, or the use of rare earth metals, or water – or pretty much anything. Economic growth itself is not a problem; the problem is consuming non-renewable resources. We don't currently have to worry about physical limits on economic growth, even if such limits might one day exist – but there are plenty of real, tangible environmental problems to tackle right now.

14

Inequality

'An imbalance between rich and poor is the oldest
and most fatal ailment of all republics.'

Plutarch

We haven't talked much about poverty and inequality yet.

I agree, and that's because neither plays a big role in standard
macroeconomic models. We still tend to deal in big economic
aggregates sloshing around like the contents of Bill Phillips's
MONIAC tanks. The issues that we've been thinking about –
of aggregate supply, aggregate demand, output and sticky
prices – don't give us much of a handle on who gets what in
the economy. But naturally you care about whether your economy features a broad middle class living in moderate comfort
or a super-rich elite sealing themselves off from widespread
misery.

Poverty and riches turn out to be tricky things to measure
when we want to compare across countries or time. Even
something apparently simple – such as the question of who
is the richest person who ever lived – becomes a rather subtle

question when you examine it. For instance, if you want to compare Bill Gates with Marcus Crassus, the Roman Republic's most famous plutocrat, you quickly find yourself comparing private planes with cellars full of wine and olive oil.

I think I care more about tackling poverty than historically ranking the über-rich.

Of course, but much the same difficulties apply at the other end of the income scale. How do we define poverty?

Well, surely poverty is the inability to afford the basics – food, clothes and shelter.

OK, so you're talking about an absolute definition of poverty, in terms of some objective measure of purchasing power. There's certainly a long tradition behind this approach. One of its pioneers was the Quaker Seebohm Rowntree, the son of a wealthy chocolate maker, Joseph Rowntree. At the end of the nineteenth century, Seebohm set about trying to measure the poverty that surrounded him in his home city, York. To that end he defined a 'poverty line' by working out how much it would cost to buy certain basics, including a helping of pease pudding with bacon on Sunday. Anyone who couldn't afford those basics was below Seebohm's poverty line.

Absolute poverty lines remain an attractive concept. The World Bank has a number of them, including the famous 'dollar a day' line defining extreme poverty – the brainwave of an economist called Martin Ravallion, who noticed in the late 1980s that several countries had poverty lines of around $370 a year. The official definition of 'a dollar' is a lot more complex than you might think. For a start, it's updated to reflect inflation, so we're really talking about what a dollar could have bought twenty-five years ago. And it adjusts for living costs, otherwise it wouldn't make much sense as a global poverty line. So the 'dollar' in Delhi isn't actually what you would get if you converted your dollar at international exchange rates. It's much less. The idea is that somebody living on the dollar-a-day standard in India would be able to buy only what you could buy with a dollar a day in America. In other words – some rice or lentils, and no shelter.[1]

That's shockingly low. You couldn't possibly survive on a dollar a day in the US.

Hundreds of millions of people really do live like this in poorer countries. But yes, we could hardly have a useful conversation about what it means to be poor in the United States if a dollar a day was our only reference point. As it happens, the US has its own set of absolute poverty lines for households of different sizes: the line was $30.52 a day in 2012 for a single person, well above what the World Bank would consider as poor.

The US definition of poverty is fifty years old: the poverty line was calculated in 1963 by a Social Security Administration researcher called Mollie Orshansky. Ms Orshansky based her estimate on much the same methods that Seebohm Rowntree had used sixty-four years before her – trying to figure out how much it would cost to feed a family a reasonable diet. (Mollie Orshansky had worked out the nutritional standards herself in the late 1940s and the 1950s, while working in the Bureau of Human Nutrition and Home Economics. She was realistic, too, about the demands her food plans made on families – in particular, that 'the housewife will be a careful shopper, a skilful cook, and a good manager who will prepare all the family's meals at home'.)[2] Orshansky's was a decent estimate given the limited resources of the time, yet since being officially adopted by the White House in 1969, the threshold has changed only to take account of inflation.

That seems reasonable enough, although it's not a lot of money.

Of course it's not a lot of money. It would hardly be a poverty line if it was a lot of money, would it? But I'd challenge your suggestion that an absolute poverty line is the right way to think about this. After all, if Seebohm Rowntree had been a US government official the United States might still be using a poverty line based on the price of pease pudding.

I was meaning to ask – what is pease pudding?

Well, exactly. You don't know, and even after reading the description on Wikipedia I have to confess I am a little hazy on the details. And yet if we had absolute poverty lines defined in 1899 and uprated for inflation, the Victorian delicacy that is pease pudding would remain in today's poverty statistics, an echo of past culinary habits. Needless to say, Seebohm Rowntree didn't think to ask about the price of electric light or indoor plumbing, both of which were luxuries in his day and thus clearly irrelevant to the question of who was poor. And naturally he could not even have imagined calculating the price of a television or internet access.

But people don't need television or internet access. They're a luxury.

Hold on. I agree that people don't need television or internet access in the same way they need food, clothes and shelter. But do you really want to lump these things in with haute cuisine, designer handbags and champagne? Imagine your child comes home from school in a wealthy country and tells you about the classmate whose family lacks the money to buy a television. Are you seriously going to say, 'Don't be silly, son, that family isn't poor'?

So are you saying we should measure poverty in relative, not absolute, terms?

It's not quite that easy, either. Crude definitions of relative poverty, such as the ones used in Europe, are pretty odd. For instance, Eurostat, the European Union's statistics agency, defines the poverty line as 60 per cent of each nation's median income. (The median income is the income of the person in the middle of the income distribution, the person poorer than half the population and richer than the other half.)

This has an odd consequence: poverty is permanent unless inequality changes. If everyone in Europe woke up tomorrow to find themselves twice as rich, European poverty rates would not budge. Conversely, poverty rates fell during the recent recession in the UK. The reason for that, obviously enough, is that the poverty line itself was falling. A family could have the same income as ever, and yet 'escape from poverty' because median incomes fell.

This won't do. The Eurostat poverty line compares the poor with middle-income households and ignores what might be happening to the rich. I think that we would be better calling a spade a spade and admitting that Eurostat is actually measuring inequality in the lower half of the income spectrum.

You're just not satisfied, are you? You dismissed the idea of an absolute poverty line and now you're dismissing the idea of a relative poverty line.

Adam Smith put his finger on the problem back in 1776. In *The Wealth of Nations*, he wrote: 'A linen shirt, for example, is, strictly speaking, not a necessity of life. The Greeks and Romans lived, I suppose, very comfortably though they had no linen. But in the present times, through the greater part of Europe, a creditable day-labourer would be ashamed to appear in public without a linen shirt.'

Smith's point is not that poverty is relative, but that it is a social condition. People don't become poor just because the median citizen receives a pay rise, whatever Eurostat may say. But they may become poor if something they cannot afford – such as a television – becomes viewed as a social essential. A person can lack the money necessary to participate in society, and that, in an important sense, is poverty.

For me, the poverty lines that make most sense are absolute poverty lines, adjusted over time to reflect social change. Appropriately enough, one of the attempts to do such work is produced by a foundation established by Seebohm Rowntree's father, Joseph. The Joseph Rowntree Foundation uses focus groups to establish what things people feel it's now necessary to have in order to take part in society – the list includes a self-catering holiday, a no-frills mobile phone, and enough money to buy a cheap suit every two or three years. Of course this is all subjective, but so is poverty. I'm not sure we will get anywhere if we believe that some expert, somewhere – even an expert as thoughtful as Mollie Orshansky or Seebohm Rowntree – is going to be able to nail down, permanently and precisely, what it means to be 'poor'.

Even if we accept the rather simpler idea of a nutrition-based absolute poverty line, there will always be complications. One obvious one is the cost of living: lower in, say, Alabama than in New York. In principle absolute poverty lines could and should take account of the cost of living, but the US poverty line does not. A second issue is how to deal with short-term loss of income. A middle manager who loses her job and is unemployed for three months before finding another well-paid position might temporarily fall below the poverty line as far as her income is concerned, but with good prospects, a credit card and savings in the bank, she won't need to live like a poor person – and she is likely to maintain much of her pre-poverty spending patterns. For this reason, some economists prefer to measure poverty not by what a household earns in a given week, month or year – but by how much money that household spends.

I understand – it's complicated. But if I can be permitted to wave all that complexity aside in favour of getting some degree of perspective – how many people are poor?

According to the official United States government definition, 15 per cent of the US population was poor in 2011. That was the highest percentage since the early 1990s, up from 12.3 per cent in 2006, just before the recession began. For all its faults, you can see one of the appeals of an absolute poverty line: if poverty goes up during recessions you are probably measuring something sensible.[3]

The European Union doesn't use a comparable poverty line, but in the year 2000, researchers at the University of York tried to work out what EU poverty rates would be as measured against US standards. They estimated poverty rates as high as 48 per cent in Portugal and as low as 6 per cent in Denmark, with France at 12 per cent, Germany at 15 per cent and the

UK at 18 per cent. Clearly, national income is a big influence on absolute poverty (Portugal is a fair bit poorer than Denmark) but so, too, is the distribution of income (France and the UK have similar average incomes, but France is more egalitarian).[4]

Globally, as we've heard, the World Bank uses a 'dollar a day' standard for extreme poverty. The number of people who are poor by this very meagre standard has been falling rapidly. One famous international development goal was to halve the proportion of the world's population living in extreme poverty between 1990 and 2015. Thanks in large part to China's growth, we've achieved that goal: in 1990, 31 per cent of the population of the developing world lived on less than a dollar a day; by 2008, the proportion had fallen to 14 per cent. It's real progress.

The picture is less encouraging in the United States. Poverty rates fell sharply throughout the 1960s, from around 22 per cent in the late 1950s to 11.1 per cent in 1973 – a figure that remains the lowest in the nation's history. It does seem pretty astonishing that a nation can enjoy decades of economic growth while making no progress on the number of people who are below the absolute poverty line – especially when the experience of the 1960s showed that rapid progress was indeed possible.

So what's the solution?

There are three broad approaches. One, to draw inspiration from a character in Tom Wolfe's *Bonfire of the Vanities*, is 'insulate, insulate, insulate' – treat the poor as something to be quarantined.

That's disgraceful.

I'm glad you think so. I'm sure you'll revise your immigration policies accordingly. A lot of people seem to have very different views of poverty in fellow citizens and poverty in foreigners.

So to turn to actual solutions, the question between the two remaining approaches is whether you wish to put resources into direct cash transfers, or into improving opportunities – for instance, improving schools, fighting crime, trying to create more decent jobs. In other words, should you help poor people, or should you make it easier for poor people to help themselves?

There is a school of thought that says that cash transfers are actually counter-productive because they encourage feckless behaviour – dependency or drug abuse. It's not at all clear that's true: generations of politicians have been happy to muddy the waters, using 'poor' and 'irresponsible' or 'troublesome' interchangeably. Recently the British government estimated that there were 120,000 'troubled families' in the country, and Prime Minister David Cameron denounced these families as racked by 'Drug addiction. Alcohol abuse. Crime.' Closer inspection revealed that the criteria for being a 'troubled family' were nothing to do with crime or drugs and everything to do with poverty, disability and unemployment.[5]

But while giving money to the poor is not the same as

giving money to a criminal underclass, it may not fix the underlying problems. Deprivation starts very early in life, so cash hand-outs will not necessarily provide a springboard to self-sufficiency. What else, then? There is a growing body of high-quality evidence based on randomised trials that providing early-years education to poor children is an extremely sensible thing to do.

The most famous such trial is the Perry Preschool Project, which provided excellent pre-schooling to a randomly selected group of deprived African-American children aged three to four during the mid-1960s.[6] (The cost, in today's money, would have been about $11,000–12,000 per child.)

When compared to a control group the Perry kids completed almost a full extra year of education, were about 45 per cent more likely to graduate from high school, and were dramatically less likely to have children out of wedlock or to become pregnant when teenagers. At the age of forty the control group were more likely than not to have spent time in prison; the rate for Perry pre-schoolers was much lower (if still high) at 28 per cent. And in middle age, the Perry kids were earning over 40 per cent more.

That's completely mind-blowing – all this because of some quality time at the age of three or four?

Yes. Just one small pilot, mind you – and we're talking about a particular quality of pre-school education for a particular group of very deprived children, at a particular time in history. But there are other good studies of quality pre-school education and it does seem to be very good indeed for children in poverty. Moreover, if you take a long-term view, it doesn't cost your government anything – in fact, it actually makes money. When you factor in the extra taxes those Perry kids ended up paying, and the money you save by not having to keep them in prison, you find that the programme paid for itself many times over.

My suggestion is to grab all the decent randomised trials you can – and commission a whole lot more – and see what you can learn about investing to level the playing field for children in poor families. Post-natal support, school reform and best-practice policing and criminal justice are all very plausible candidates for being effective social interventions. And to be honest, you won't get to run a randomised trial for monetary policy or stimulus spending, so you might as well enjoy serious evidence while you can get it.

One other thing. There is a newly fashionable scheme out there called the 'conditional cash transfer', pioneered in Latin America. The idea is to give cash to poor families on condition that they do something you'd like them to do – for example, send their children to school, or get them vaccinated. The attractions of the scheme are obvious: you get the cool social interventions, such as pre-school, and you also get to give money to poor families while ensuring that they behave themselves. The disadvantages are pretty obvious, too: children in extremely dysfunctional families may need help most of all, and yet be excluded. Perhaps it's worth a few properly evaluated pilots?

Duly noted. But we began this conversation talking about inequality and I'd still like to understand what's going on there. Inequality is rising, isn't it?

That depends on how you measure it. The richest countries in the world keep on getting richer, while the poorest countries in the world are, if anything, getting poorer. But that simplistic benchmark for inequality has some serious flaws. For a start, it glosses over what's going on in countries that are neither the richest nor the poorest. China has been getting less poor at an astonishing rate, for example. A measure of inequality which gives poverty-mired Burundi (population 8 million) the same weight as once-poor, now-booming China (population 1300 million) will show that inequality increased dramatically between 1950 and 2000, but has eased off a little since then. But a more sensible measure of inequality which weights countries according to their population shows unambiguous progress: inequality fell gradually between 1950 and 1990, and then fell extremely quickly after 1990.

That's great news – and a bit of a surprise. Is there a catch?

There is a catch, and it's to do with the other flaw of comparing inequality between nations – it ignores what's happening to inequality inside countries. The estimates I've given you so far – calculated by Branko Milanovic of the World Bank – compare average incomes for each country.[7] But imagine that the United States became a socialist utopia, redistributing money from Bill Gates and Warren Buffett and all the hedge fund multi-millionaires until everybody in the country had the same income. That wouldn't make any difference to a simple measure of global inequality that merely compared national averages, because the US would be as rich as before.

When Milanovic tries to adjust for inequality within countries, he finds that global inequality was rising until around the end of the twentieth century. Inequality appears now to be falling – probably for the first time since the industrial revolution – but the fall is quite modest. As we know that simple inequality between countries is falling rapidly, logic tells us that inequality *inside* many countries must be increasing, also fairly rapidly. That indeed is what's happening; measuring the two at the same time, they almost cancel each other out.

Hmm. Should we be more worried about inequality between countries, or within countries?

Interesting question. You might argue that inequality between countries is more worrying because it can't possibly be meritocratic. Being born in an average household in, say, Zimbabwe or Eritrea pretty much dooms you to poverty unless you can emigrate, no matter how much of a genius you are. Being born in poverty in the US or the UK, if you're smart and have the right character, you have a chance of overcoming the disadvantage. So you might argue that inequality between nations is of a more pernicious kind. On the other hand, you might argue that inequality within a nation is more socially corrosive and easier to fix.

So let's focus on this question of inequality within nations – it's where the trend is in the wrong direction, anyway. What's the story?

Depends where we look and how we measure. One interesting approach is to look at the three great developing countries, Brazil, China and India. Often lumped together, the countries are hugely different in many ways – not least with regard to what is happening to inequality.

Start with Brazil. Brazil is a notoriously unequal society. The CIA's *World Factbook* reported that the Gini coefficient for Brazil – a common measure of inequality – was 61 per cent in 1998.[8] Given that a Gini of 100 per cent is a single person making all the money in the country, topping 60 per cent is pretty stark. For comparison, France's Gini was 33 per cent, Finland's 27 per cent, and it was 34 per cent in the UK and 45 per cent in the US.

But here's the thing: Brazil's Gini is now down to 52 per cent. That's still high but it's a big fall, a quarter of the way to becoming ultra-egalitarian Finland in just fifteen years. It shows that in the right circumstances inequality can be tackled: Lula da Silva, the Brazilian President from 2003 to 2010, was regarded as a revolutionary firebrand when elected, but turned into a pragmatist who was happy to court international business investment, yet was keen to redistribute some of the rewards of Brazil's commodity boom.

India is a different case, with a Gini index in the high 30s both in the late 1990s and more recently. Despite a few very successful entrepreneurs – and the entrepreneur Mukesh Ambani's notorious billion-dollar house, towering the equivalent of forty storeys over Mumbai – there simply isn't enough money in India yet for it to be very unequal. That may change, if China is anything to go by.

China – still ostensibly a communist country – is a study in income contrasts. The *Factbook* puts the Gini coefficient there at 48 per cent. That is already higher than the level in the United States, and given that China is still much poorer than the US, such income inequality implies tremendous hardship for poorer families. A more recent study found a Gini coefficient of 61, which if true is pretty serious.[9] No wonder China's leaders are nervous about social unrest, even though the country is still growing very quickly indeed.

It's a socialist country. Why on earth has inequality been allowed to reach such levels?

Two reasons. One is the attitude summed up by China's first great reformist, Deng Xiaoping, who took power in 1978 following the end of the Maoist era. One of his much-quoted maxims was '*Rang yi bu fen ren xian fu qi lai*,' or 'Let some people get rich first'. There is some sense in this. China's growth model has been very experimental, loosening different restrictions on different industries in different parts of the country – and in particular creating globalisation-friendly industrial zones on the coast. It is almost inevitable that such experiments, if successful, would produce winners and losers. Not everywhere can develop at the same rate, and in the process of creative destruction many people will miss out or lose out. In fairness, growth rates inland have also been high – just not as high, and not for as long, as at the coast.

The second reason is a little more sinister. Almost one in ten of China's richest thousand people sit in the National People's Congress – a body of almost three thousand law-makers. Their average net worth is four times the average net worth of the richest politicians in the US Congress, despite the fact that the US itself is a far wealthier nation. Many people worry that the US is subject to too much influence from plutocrats; if that is true then the situation in China looks even worse.[10]

But this does raise the question of inequality in rich countries. What's the picture there?

After decades of falling, or at least low and stable, inequality within rich countries, inequality in Anglophone nations has now been rising for about twenty-five years. The most dramatic symptom of that is a dramatic increase in the income enjoyed by the very richest – the top 1 per cent, for instance, or even the top 0.1 per cent. You might think that focusing on these few multi-millionaires is tokenism – a distraction. But it seems to be significant.

In the United States, for instance, average incomes grew by 13.1 per cent between 1993 and 2011. That's not a lot of growth, to be honest, over the course of nearly two decades. But what's alarming is that if you look at growth in average incomes for the poorest 99 per cent – that is, everyone from the destitute up to families making less than about $370,000 – the growth in average incomes is just 5.8 per cent over the course of eighteen years, an extremely low figure.

The difference between 13.1 per cent (the growth in average income) and 5.8 per cent (the growth in average income once you remove the rich) is huge.[11] The salaries of the most highly paid are now so high that it's no longer a question of symbolism: they are having a real impact on the shape of the economy.

There's a similar story to tell about income growth for the top 0.1 per cent, and it's not purely an American phenomenon – although using top income shares as a measure, inequality is higher in the US, and has increased more quickly, than in other major economies. There is something curiously Anglophone about the phenomenon, though: the growth in the share of national income accruing to the top 1 per cent of earners has also risen sharply in the UK and Canada, and to a lesser extent in New Zealand and Australia. But look at France, Germany, the Netherlands, Switzerland or Japan and you'd be hard pressed to discern any increase at all. This does suggest that the rise in inequality at the top of the income distribution reflects some kind of cultural or political force, or at least that pure impersonal economics is not the sole explanation.[12]

Do we know why inequality is rising in the Anglophone nations, then?

A few years ago the journalist Timothy Noah conducted an exhaustive review of all the ideas out there, including 'race, gender, or the breakdown of the nuclear family . . . immigration, the technology boom, federal government policy, the decline of labor unions, international trade, whether the ultra wealthy are to blame, and what role the decline of K-12 education has played'.[13] It gives you a sense of just how many different possible explanations are in play. And of course, if we observe that – say – the political environment in Anglophone countries is less conducive to trade unions than it used to be, and that businesses have become more eager to pay so much to corporate executives and Wall Street masters of the universe, then that just shifts the need for an explanation up a level – why did these developments affect Anglophone countries more?

For what it's worth, I think the most significant trend of all is probably an unholy alliance of indifferent schools and technological change. Economists tend to place a lot of weight on something called skill-biased technological change, or SBTC for short. In a nutshell this is the idea that sixty years ago you needed to be able to shovel stuff around; thirty years ago you needed to be able to control the mechanical shovel; now you need to be able to fix the robot shovel when it breaks down. Because of changing technology a skilled worker can do more than ever, while an unskilled worker is becoming something of a liability. This is why schools matter. But if you look at the OECD's 'Pisa' rankings of student achievement, you'll see that the US and the UK are outside the top fifteen in science and reading – and outside the top twenty-five in maths.

In a striking contrast, British and American universities consistently dominate rankings of the best higher education institutions in the world. It's easy to see how inequality might emerge from this dichotomy: the world's two most unequal wealthy economies offer a mediocre school education to the masses and an outstanding university education to an elite.

If this is right, then presumably inequality will escalate as the speed of technological change increases.

It's possible, although in theory future technological changes might favour less skilled workers again. This is all related to the conundrum we addressed in the last chapter, when we considered whether a zero-growth economy with technological change would inevitably lead to mass unemployment.

I will say that we shouldn't overestimate the threats of technology. It may have destroyed many jobs (for example, through the mechanisation of agriculture) but it has also created new ones (for example, web design). It's reasonable to expect that this trend will continue. But it is at least conceivable that in the future, many people will have almost no economic value at all: there will be nothing they can do that a robot cannot do more quickly, safely, cheaply and reliably. Some humans – perhaps most humans – will not be able to compete while earning any kind of living wage. All the economic returns would go to the owners of capital.

It seems unlikely that this is a world most of us would want to live in, and there would surely come a point where we would have to abandon many of the economic institutions that have got us this far; perhaps we'll have to organise society so that everybody, at birth, is given her own inalienable portfolio of shares in the robot manufacturers.

Still, a future of everyone relaxing while being pampered by our robot servants seems a long way off. Let's close by thinking about what the nearer-term future of economics might hold.

15

The future of macroeconomics

'Ultimately macro is an empirical subject. [It cannot indefinitely remain] impervious to the facts.'

Professor Hyun Song Shin[1]

The recent crisis must have caused some soul-searching for macroeconomists, right? None of them saw it coming.

That's true, although forecasting is not the economist's main job. Unfortunately, economists have managed to stereotype themselves as bad forecasters because investment firms have realised that they can get some publicity by sending someone called a 'chief economist' to the studios of Bloomberg Television, where said chief economist will opine about whether shares will go up or down. Most academic economists don't even try to forecast, because they know that forecasts of complex systems are extremely difficult – if anything, rather than being overconfident in their forecasts, they're too eager to dismiss forecasting as an activity for fools and frauds.

Keynes famously remarked, 'If economists could manage to get themselves thought of as humble, competent people, on a level with dentists, that would be splendid!' It's a good joke but it's not just a joke; you don't expect your dentist to be able to forecast the pattern of tooth decay but you expect that she will be able to give you good practical advice on dental health and to intervene to fix problems when they occur. That is what we should demand from economists: useful advice about how to keep the economy working well, and solutions when the economy malfunctions.

We're several years on from the banking crisis now, and it doesn't exactly feel like the solutions have been impressive.

You have a point. When you look at the most exciting, innovative work coming out of economics today, it's pretty much all from microeconomists, not macroeconomists. Think of Al Roth's work on market design, where he uses computer-based algorithms to allocate children to school places, young doctors to their first hospital jobs, and kidney donors to compatible patients. Economists such as Paul Milgrom, Hal Varian and Paul Klemperer are scoring notable successes in auction design, from Google Ads to lucrative spectrum auctions to efforts to support the banking system without giving massive hand-outs to banks. John List, Esther Duflo and others are designing economic experiments to reveal hidden truths about human behaviour. These economists are much more like dentists – or doctors, or engineers. They solve problems.

And macroeconomists don't?

We shouldn't be too harsh on them. As I hope you've picked up by now, macroeconomics is hard. You've got ten billion product varieties, seven billion people, countless unobservable transactions. The economy is shaped by psychology, history, culture, unforeseeable new technologies, geological and climatic events, computer traders too quick for humans to perceive, and much else. It is a dizzying, imponderable problem. No wonder we struggle.

But the second reason why we don't have macroeconomic dentists is that, perhaps in response to the complexity of the problem, the discipline has intellectually isolated itself. All academic disciplines have a tendency to think in silos, but in macroeconomics the problem seems to be particularly acute.

Remember that famous claim by Keynes (again) that 'the master-economist must possess a rare combination of gifts . . . He must be a mathematician, historian, statesman, philosopher – in some degree. He must understand symbols and speak in words. He must contemplate the particular in terms of the general, and touch abstract and concrete in the same flight of thought. He must study the present in the light of the past for the purposes of the future. No part of man's nature or his institutions must lie entirely outside his regard.'

Over the past forty years, academic macroeconomics has turned its back on this job description.

Instead of stretching out to grab any methodological tool that might shed light on the economy, modern macroeconomics has narrowed its focus. There is a limited range of assumptions and modelling techniques that are regarded as publishable in the top journals. Macroeconomic models have become elegant and logically sophisticated, but suffer a serious disconnection from reality. The thinking has been that logical consistency must come first, and hopefully the models will start to look realistic eventually. This is not entirely ridiculous – Robert Lucas's critique of the Phillips curve and the chastening stagflation of the 1970s showed economists that it wasn't enough merely to draw conclusions from the data, because the data could change dramatically. But four decades on from the 'rational expectations' revolution, there are good reasons to believe that macroeconomics is failing to incorporate some important perspectives.

For example?

Three examples spring to mind: banking, behavioural economics and complexity theory.

Banking has been left out of most macroeconomic models for many decades – this has been true of both the Keynesian and classical sides of modern macroeconomics. As with so many of the mis-steps of academia, this wasn't initially an unreasonable move. Banks are extremely complicated and yet their end product seems rather simple: they form a bridge between people who want to save money and people who want to borrow it. Why not, then, simply wave a magic wand and assume that this job is done, and done well, and get on with trying to understand more interesting matters?

The Great Depression was triggered by a banking crisis, which might have been regarded as a warning sign not to remove banking from macroeconomic models. This warning sign was ignored for two reasons: first, governments introduced deposit insurance, which made bank runs far less likely and seemed to have fixed banking's most obvious fragility; second, the Great Depression became an ever more distant memory. For macroeconomists to worry about banking started to feel like a military strategist worrying about cavalry charges – interesting but a historical curiosity.

Well, this particular cavalry charge happened anyway, and it turned out to be a massacre. The macroeconomists were wrong – and look how much damage was done as a result.

Let's be careful. Much as I would love to blame the macro-economists for everything – I am a microeconomist myself – keeping the banking system safe was not their responsibility. It was the job of a bunch of politicians, bankers, lawyers, accountants and microeconomists – and as I argue in my previous book, *Adapt*, we probably should have been listening a lot more to safety engineers and organisational behaviour experts.

The flaw in macroeconomics was that when the banking crisis hit, the macroeconomic mainstream didn't have good models of what the economic consequences might be, although casual empiricism suggested that they wouldn't be pretty. As a result it was hard to say much that was authoritative about how central banks should cushion the blow, and whether governments should be reaching for stimulus or austerity. Was the banking crisis best thought of as a demand shock, leading to a Keynesian recession? Or a supply shock, producing a classical recession? Or was that whole intellectual apparatus useless?

Worse, many microeconomists argue that the high priests of macroeconomics have been slow to respond even after the fact – reluctant to allow the banking sector into their models and, in some cases, reluctant even to acknowledge that the crisis demands any intellectual response. The truth is that even if macroeconomists had leapt into action as the crisis hit, the intellectual project of understanding the interaction between banking and the economy as a whole is a difficult one.[2]

Your second example, behavioural economics, isn't such a challenge, is it? It's been around for quite a while.

Yes, behavioural economics, a kind of fusion of economics and psychology, has made big inroads into economic thought in the last fifteen years. Daniel Kahneman, a psychologist who helped to create the field, was awarded the Nobel memorial prize in economics; George Akerlof, another laureate, is an evangelist for behavioural economics, as is Robert Shiller, a finance expert famous for his demonstration that both the dot-com bubble and the housing bubble were – well, bubbles. Matthew Rabin, a younger behavioural economist, received the John Bates Clark medal for economists under the age of forty – it has often been a precursor to a Nobel. Another luminary, Richard Thaler, most famous as the co-author of *Nudge*, has long had an influential pulpit in the form of a regular feature in one of the leading journals, the *Journal of Economic Perspectives*. Microeconomists were initially sceptical, and many remain sceptical. But sceptical or not, they have paid attention and either embraced behavioural economics or criticised it.

But macroeconomists? They seem to have ignored behavioural economics almost entirely. Robert Shiller told me that while the microeconomists would show up to argue when he gave seminars on behavioural finance, the macroeconomists just haven't showed up at all.

Perhaps macroeconomics has nothing to gain from behavioural economics.

That seems most unlikely. Behavioural economics is a young field and has its problems – artificial laboratory settings, small samples, and the difficulty of turning a grab-bag of behavioural surprises into some workable theory of human behaviour. But the idea that insights about actual human behaviour have no relevance to the economy as a whole is far-fetched.

We've already seen three absolutely key behavioural questions force themselves into macroeconomics because there was no way to keep them out. First, sticky wages and sticky prices: one of the most obvious reasons that wages and prices might stick is because people acquire some sense of the 'just' price, and become highly resistant to change; they might also confuse nominal and real price changes. Understanding how and why this happens may be fundamental to understanding recessions – it's certainly key to the way that modern Keynesians think about recessions.

Second, efficiency wages: as we saw in the case of Ford's five-dollar day, there may be an incentive for employers to pay much more than the market-clearing wage, which means there will be people who want jobs and can't get them. It's possible to produce models of efficiency wages that don't rely on psychological explanations, but psychology does provide some intuitive accounts of why efficiency wages might be good for profits. If sticky prices are central to understanding recessions, then efficiency wages are central to understanding unemployment. These are hardly irrelevant subjects.

Third, the question of how people form expectations is vital. We've seen how Robert Lucas turned economics upside down, and he argued that it made most sense to assume that people formed rational expectations. This led to a game theorist's vision of macroeconomics, and was certainly more logical than the careless or ad hoc modelling of expectations that had gone before. But are rational expectations really the best approach? Understanding expectations is fundamental to understanding the impact of new monetary and fiscal policies, but the project is a difficult one – led by Thomas Sargent, a Nobel laureate in economics, who began by analysing models based on rational expectations but has broadened his horizons to incorporate decision-makers whose knowledge is far more limited.

In each case – sticky prices, efficiency wages, expectations – the psychological perspective that emerges from behavioural economics has proved itself highly relevant to a central problem of macroeconomics: recessions, unemployment, and the impact of policy changes. In each case, macroeconomists have done their best to give the psychological perspective as small a role as they possibly can. Even if the behavioural economists turn out to be wrong about everything that matters, surely the subject cannot be ignored. It deserves a rebuttal at the very least – and probably a great deal more than that.

Surely psychology plays a role in determining share prices, house prices and business investment?

Possibly. John Maynard Keynes – yet again! – thought that we couldn't model consumer spending or business investment based on rational calculation of future rewards. The future was just too imponderable. Instead, investment would be determined by what he called 'animal spirits', a more emotional, intuitive sense of whether the time was ripe to take risks. Recently, George Akerlof and Robert Shiller wrote a book with just that title, *Animal Spirits*, with the aim of putting psychology back into macroeconomic analysis. It has not been easy to persuade macroeconomists to pay much attention – and to be fair to them, taking small, low-stakes laboratory experiments and applying the lessons to major financial investments is not an easy task.

And what about complexity theory?

If behavioural economics attempts to introduce more psychological realism into macroeconomics, complexity theory tends to push the other way. (I say 'tends' because complexity theory means different things to different people.)[3] Many complexity models try to expand dramatically the number of agents in the model – from one or two 'representative' agents to thousands or even millions of interacting units. While traditional economic models contain equations that are simply solved mathematically, complexity models are like simulated ant colonies inside a computer; no two runs of the simulation will produce quite the same result. The downside of this modelling approach is that the individual agents in the model tend to be extremely simple; read 'stupid'. Understanding the stock market or the housing market becomes more like understanding how sand forms in piles or how ice freezes. But the hope is that what we lose in psychological realism, we gain in our understanding of system dynamics.

There'd be no shortage of intellectual adventures in macroeconomics, then, for a modern-day Bill Phillips.

Indeed not. You might have expected that Bill would have been dragged into those 1970s debates about the collapse of the Phillips curve and the Lucas critique. As we discussed in Chapter 11, the disappointment over the Phillips curve nudged macroeconomics into a highly mathematical trajectory, and the Lucas critique made economists nervous about relying too heavily on empirical correlations.

But Bill Phillips had turned his attention elsewhere entirely: to China. In the wartime prison camp, Phillips had studied Chinese, learning enough of it that he eventually became a prison-camp instructor and would read classic Chinese novels. But China was, by the mid-1960s, one of the very poorest places on the planet. Still, Bill felt that it was a place that could not be ignored and he was determined to study China and its economy. In 1967, he moved to the Australian National University in Canberra, on condition that he could spend half his time working on China. He didn't have long, alas: he suffered a debilitating stroke in 1969 and a fatal one in 1975; when he died, he was only sixty years old.

It feels like a sad end.

It was untimely, to be sure. But Phillips's final career moves were telling. At a time when macroeconomics was becoming ever more abstract, describing the evolution of an idealised economy at no particular time and in no particular place, Bill was still fascinated by the challenge of a vast, underdeveloped economy with a rich culture. He could solve differential equations but he never lost sight of the fact that economics is about people.

And Phillips was also, right to the end, fascinated by the endless complexities of system dynamics – the way economies could oscillate, and how they might be stabilised. Curiously, the task facing macroeconomics in incorporating the lessons of the crisis has a recent parallel in engineering, in the shape of London's famous Millennium Bridge.

When it opened, it was the first new crossing of the Thames to be built for over a century, and it provided a beautiful walkway between the Tate Modern gallery and St Paul's Cathedral. But a problem very quickly developed – the bridge, packed with people eager to try it out, began to wobble alarmingly from side to side. Imagine laying a Slinky flat on the ground and gently moving one end from side to side to send a horizontal ripple along the Slinky's length, and you get a sense of how the bridge was moving. It was disconcerting; the bridge was closed down within two days until the problem could be diagnosed and fixed.

It turned out that the bridge and the pedestrians were synchronising with each other in an unexpected way. When the bridge wobbled very slightly, the pedestrians adjusted their gait. People walking on the bridge started to walk like ice skaters, pushing their feet out to either side as they tried to keep their balance. And of course, they did so in sync with each other, responding to the bridge's movement. This synchronised ice-skating motion was enough to increase the wobble of the bridge. The bridge might be fine for a while, but as soon as the slightest movement began to occur, the crowd would respond to the wobble and the wobble would respond to the crowd.

The wobbly bridge is interesting for two reasons. The first is that it shows how difficult it is to solve real-world problems using pure theory. Many people have a sense that engineering is founded on the rock-solid laws of physics, while economics is a castle built on sand. The truth is that while engineers do have the laws of physics to rely on, they are often caught out once reality intervenes. Sometimes the results are tragic: when the innovative Malpasset dam in the south of France cracked thanks to inadequate geological modelling, nearly four hundred people died. Sometimes they are delicious: the award-winning Kemper Arena in Kansas City collapsed, with no loss of life, just twenty-four hours after hosting the American Institute of Architects Convention.[4]

The trouble is not the fact that engineers don't understand the laws of physics – it's that actually modelling them in a world full of snowdrifts, geological clay seams and self-synchronising pedestrians is a difficult affair. And if structural engineers can sometimes be caught out like this, we should not entirely blame macroeconomists if the economy remains an unruly subject of study.

The second reason that the wobbly bridge is interesting is that one of the men who worked out what had gone wrong with the bridge was a Cambridge engineering lecturer by the name of Allan McRobie – the same Allan McRobie who painstakingly rebuilt Cambridge's version of Bill Phillips's MONIAC, and turned it from a museum curiosity back into a fully functioning hydraulic computer.[5] McRobie is like Phillips: an engineer with eclectic interests. Bill Phillips, remember, started as a tinkerer, a mechanic. Even leaving aside the crocodile hunting and the wartime heroics, he became a hydraulic engineer, a constructor of covert electronics, a sociologist, an economist and a pioneer in computing. He was interested in the details of how things worked, and always looking for inspiration in new fields of study. And rather than wanting to lock himself in an ivory tower, Bill Phillips wanted to solve practical problems.

And perhaps that is no bad example for us all.

Resources

If you've made it this far, there are some excellent economics resources available to tempt you.

If you like podcasts, try the superb *Planet Money* from NPR (http://www.npr.org/blogs/money/) which tells stories about economic and business issues from across the world.

Yoram Bauman and Grady Klein have written the *Cartoon Guide to Macroeconomics*, much more fun than the textbooks. Timothy Taylor's *The Instant Economist* also contains chapters which offer a good jumping-off point for the macroeconomics scholar.

And the ever-changing debates about economics and economic policy are well covered by a host of economics blogs, most of which are entirely free. Start by following my Twitter feed – @timharford – and you'll soon discover links to what I think is worth reading.

Acknowledgements

Thanks to my colleagues at the *Financial Times* and the BBC – working with them is a great pleasure and a constant source of ideas. I should particularly thank Alec Russell, whose invitation to write a new column in 2011 helped me develop the dialogue style of writing I used in this book.

Thanks too to everyone at Little, Brown, particularly Iain Hunt and Tim Whiting, for their confident support of this book – and to my wonderful publishers, editors and publicists across the world, who have developed such an amazing reach from Spain to Korea, Estonia to Brazil.

Sally Holloway, Zoe Pagnamenta, and a team of many others have been superb agents.

Every time I acknowledge those who have helped me I find myself commenting that Andrew Wright is a genius. It's still true.

At Oxford, Paul Klemperer, Anthony Courakis, John Vickers, Simon Wren-Lewis, Michael Horvath and David Hendry all provided advice, encouragement or comments. Tony, of course, also provided three years of patient and memorable macro-economics tuition when I was an undergraduate. I am grateful to all of them and I hope the results don't disappoint them too deeply.

I am indebted to the Reserve Bank of New Zealand and to

Bill Phillips's sister, Carol Somervell, for sharing photos and archive material about Bill; and also to Allan Sleeman, for sharing an unpublished monograph on the life of Bill Phillips.

Above all, my love and thanks to the ever-wonderful Fran Monks. Go team!

One final acknowledgement – to my readers. Thank you; I am lucky to have you.

Washington DC, March 2013

Notes

1 Two excellent sources for Bill Phillips are A.G. Sleeman, 'The Phillips Curve: A Rushed Job?', *Journal of Economic Perspectives* 25:1 (Winter 2011), and 'Bill Phillips' War and his Notorious Pass Degree', *Economic Record* 86:274 (September 2010). Alan Bollard gave a biographical lecture on 16 July 2008 with some delightful details; it is available on the YouTube channel of the Reserve Bank of New Zealand. Allan McRobie demonstrates the Phillips machine in a lecture, 'The Phillips Machine Demonstrated by Allan McRobie': http://www.sms.cam.ac.uk/media/1094078. A short BBC Radio 4 documentary on the machine, 'Electronic Brains: Water on the Brain', is also available: http://www.bbc.co.uk/radio4/science/electronicbrains.shtml.

2 Peter Temin, 'Great Depression', in Steven N. Durlauf and Lawrence E. Blume (eds), *The New Palgrave Dictionary of Economics*, Vol. 3 (2nd edn, Basingstoke: Palgrave Macmillan, 2008).

3 Unpublished research by the UK Cabinet Office Behavioural Insight Team, based on author's interview with Owain Service of the BIT, 13 February 2013.

1 The economy: a user's manual

1 David Blanchflower, David Bell, Alberto Montagnoli and Mirko Moro, 'The Effect of Macroeconomic Shocks on Well-Being', Conference Paper, March 2013, http://www.bos.frb.org/employment2013/papers/Blanchflower_Session5%20.pdf

2 The babysitting recession

1 See Joan Sweeney and Richard James Sweeney, 'Monetary Theory and the Great Capitol Hill Baby Sitting Co-op Crisis', *Journal of Money, Credit, and Banking*, February 1977, Vol. 9, Issue 1, pp. 86–9; Paul Krugman, 'Baby-sitting the economy', *Slate*, 14 August 1998: http://www.slate.com/articles/business/the_dismal_science/1998/08/babysitting_the_economy.single.html

2 This example is taken directly – after adjustment for inflation – from Daniel Kahneman, Jack L. Knetsch and Richard H. Thaler, 'Fairness as a Constraint on Profit Seeking: Entitlements in the Market', *American Economic Review* 76 (1986).

3 On Coca-Cola, see Daniel Levy and Andrew Young, 'The Real Thing: Nominal Price Rigidity of the Nickel Coke, 1886–1959', MPRA Paper 1046 (University Library of Munich, 2004); on supermarket pricing, see Daniel Levy *et al.*, 'The Magnitude of Menu Costs: Direct Evidence from Large U.S. Supermarket Chains', *Quarterly Journal of Economics* 112:3 (August 1997), pp. 791–825; and also see Daniel Levy, 'Price Rigidity and Flexibility: New Empirical Evidence', *Managerial and Decision Economics* 28:7 (2007), pp. 639–47. The Coca-Cola story was also covered with elegance by the Planet Money podcast, Episode 416, 'Why The Price of Coke Didn't Change for 70 Years'.

4 This story is told by Tyler Cowen and Alex Tabarrok in their textbook, *Modern Principles of Economics*, (Worth, 2012) p. 573.

3 Money, money, money

1 Jim Reid, 'Money to Burn', *Observer*, 25 September 1994.

2 At the time of writing, the footage is on YouTube, starting at about four minutes, 'K Foundation Burn a Million Quid': http://www.youtube.com/ watch?v=i6q4n5TQnpA.

3 Yap is becoming famous amongst monetary economists. Good sources are Michael F. Bryan, 'Island Money', Federal Reserve Bank of Cleveland, 1 February 2004: http://www.cleveland

fed.org/research/commentary/2004/0201.pdf; 'Road to Riches', BBC News website: http://news.bbc.co.uk/hi/english/static/road_to_riches/prog2/tharngan.stm; 'The Invention of Money', *This American Life*, Episode 423, January 2011: http://www.this americanlife.org/radio-archives/episode/423/transcript

4 Timothy Taylor *The Instant Economist* (London: Plume, 2012) p. 136

5 'The Invention of Money', *This American Life*, Episode 423, January 2011: http://www.thisamericanlife.org/radio-archives/episode/423/transcript

6 In addition to the excellent *This American Life* show, see Leslie Evans, 'How Brazil Beat Hyperinflation', UCLA International website, 22 February 2002: http://www.econ.puc-rio.br/gfranco/How%20Brazil%20Beat%20Hyperinflation.htm

4 Just enough inflation

1 On the theme of 'central banks have superpowers', I strongly recommend *Planet Money*'s podcast 'Europe Turns on the Bat Signal', 6 December 2011. You'll hear that the US Federal Reserve is like Superman, while the European Central Bank is the darker, moodier and more recalcitrant Batman: http://www.npr.org/blogs/money/2011/12/06/143231194/the-tuesday-podcast-europe-turns-on-the-bat-signal.

2 Steve Hanke and Nicholas Krus, 'World Hyperinflations', Cato Institute Working Paper, 15 August, 2012: http://www.cato.org/sites/cato.org/files/pubs/pdf/WorkingPaper-8.pdf

5 Stimulus

1 Dylan Matthews, 'Did the Stimulus Work? A Review of the Nine Best Studies on the Subject', *Washington Post Wonkblog*, 24 April 2011. http://www.washingtonpost.com/blogs/wonkblog/post/did-the-stimulus-work-a-review-of-the-nine-best-studies-on-the-subject/2011/08/16/gIQAThbibJ_blog.html

2 I worked on the Reinhart and Rogoff story with my BBC

colleague Ruth Alexander. Ruth Alexander, 'Reinhart, Rogoff ... and Herndon: The Student Who Caught Out the Profs', *BBC News Magazine*, 20 April 2013. http://www.bbc.co.uk/news/magazine-22223190

3 Ethan Ilzetzki, Enrique G. Mendoza and Carlos A.Vegh, 'How Big are Fiscal Multipliers?', Centre for Economic Policy Research Policy Insight 39, October 2009: http://www.cepr.org/pubs/PolicyInsights/PolicyInsight39.pdf

4 Merchandise trade data is for 2011, drawn from the World Development Indicators database: http://data.worldbank.org/indicator/TG.VAL.TOTL.GD.ZS

6 The prison-camp recession

1 R.A. Radford, 'The Economic Organisation of a POW Camp', *Economica* 12:48 (November 1945).

2 In a famous interview with *Time* magazine in 1968, Friedman commented that 'in one sense, we are all Keynesians now; in another, no one is a Keynesian any longer'. He elaborated: 'We all use the Keynesian language and apparatus; none of us any longer accepts the initial Keynesian conclusions.' For more discussion see Roger Garrison, 'Is Milton Friedman a Keynesian?': http://www.auburn.edu/~garriro/fm2friedman.htm; and Nicholas Wapshott, 'A Lovefest between Milton Friedman and J.M. Keynes': http://www.thedailybeast.com/articles/2012/07/30/nicholas-wapshott-a-lovefest-between-milton-friedman-and-j-m-keynes.html

7 Output gaps

1 Paul Krugman, *End This Depression Now!* (W.W. Norton 2012) Also speeches by Ben Broadbent and David Miles: David Miles, 'Monetary Policy and the Damaged Economy', 24 May 2012: http://www.bankofengland.co.uk/publications/Documents/speeches/2012/ speech576.pdf; Ben Broadbent, 'Productivity and the Allocation of Resources': http://www.bankofengland.co.uk/

publications/Documents/speeches/2012/speech599.pdf; Federal Reserve data: http://www.federalreserve.gov/releases/g17/current/table11.htm

8 The invention of unemployment

1 Henry Ford quotation from the *Zanesville Sunday Times-Signal* (15 March 1931), reported in Wikiquote, accessed 18 December 2012: http://en.wikiquote.org/wiki/Henry_Ford

2 For more historical detail on Ford and the efficiency wage hypothesis, see Daniel Raff and Lawrence Summers, 'Did Henry Ford Pay Efficiency Wages?', NBER Working Paper 2101 (October 1989).

3 Christopher Pissarides, Royal Economic Society Public Lecture, London, 22 November 2012.

4 Department for Work and Pensions, 'Impacts and Costs and Benefits of the Future Jobs Fund', November 2012: http://statistics.dwp.gov.uk/asd/asd1/adhoc_analysis/2012/impacts_costs_benefits_fjf.pdf

5 Crépon, Bruno, Esther Duflo, Marc Gurgend, Roland Rathelot and Philippe Zamora (2013), 'Do Labour Market Policies Have Displacement Effects? Evidence from a Clustered Randomized Experiment', *Quarterly Journal of Economics*, 128(2).

6 Samuel Bentolila, Juan Dolado and Juan Francisco Jimeno, 'The Spanish Labour Market: A Very Costly Insider-Outsider Divide', 20 January 2012: http://www.voxeu.org/article/jobless-spain-what-can-be-done-about-insider-outsider-divide

9 Boss-o-nomics

1 John van Reenen, Royal Economic Society Public Lecture, London, 2 December 2010: http://cep.lse.ac.uk/textonly/_new/staff/vanreenen/pdf/res_2010_3.pdf; Nick Bloom, 'Does Management Matter? Evidence from India', Stanford Working Paper: http://www.stanford.edu/~nbloom/DMM.pdf. Further details on the Indian study can be found in Ray Fisman and Tim Sullivan, *The Org: The Underlying Logic of the Office* (New York:

Twelve Books, 2013).

2   Kathy Fogel, Randall Morck and Bernard Yeung, 'Big Business
     Stability and Economic Growth: Is What's Good for General
     Motors Good for America?', *Journal of Financial Economics* 89:1
     (July 2008), pp. 83–108.

10   The sirens of macroeconomics

1   A.G. Sleeman, 'Retrospectives: The Phillips Curve: A Rushed
     Job?', *Journal of Economic Perspectives* 25:1 (Winter 2011).
2   Thomas Sargent, 'Rational Expectations and the Reconstruc-
     tion of Macroeconomics', *Federal Reserve Bank of Minneapolis
     Quarterly Review* (Summer 1980): http://www.minneapolisfed.
     org/research/qr/qr434.pdf

11   The cult of GNP

1   Richard A. Easterlin, 'Kuznets, Simon (1901–1985)', in Durlauf
     and Blume (eds), *The New Palgrave Dictionary of Economics*.
2   Robert Costanza *et al.*, 'The Value of the World's Ecosystem
     Services and Natural Capital', *Nature* 387 (1997), p. 259.
3   Carl Bialik, 'Putting a Number on Happiness – The Numbers
     Guy', *Wall Street Journal*, 20 July 2006: http://online.wsj.com/
     article/SB115331471730311053.html

12   Happynomics

1   For my own writings on the subject in the *Financial Times* see
     'Happiness: A Measure of Cheer', *Financial Times*, 27 December
     2010; 'The Difficult Question of Happiness', 14 April 2012;
     'Happiness Rethink', 22 October 2010.
2   Michael Blastland, 'Why It's Hard to Measure Happiness', *BBC
     News Magazine*, 16 November 2010: http://www.bbc.co.uk/
     news/magazine-11765401
3   Angus Deaton, 'The Financial Crisis and the Well-Being

of Americans', *Oxford Economic Papers* (2011) http://oep. oxfordjournals.org/content/early/2011/11/02/oep.gpr051. full.pdf

4 Richard Easterlin, 'Does Economic Growth Improve the Human Lot? Some Empirical Evidence', *Nations and Households in Economic Growth* 89 (1974) pp. 89–125.

5 Will Wilkinson, 'In Pursuit of Happiness Research: Is It Reliable? What Does It Imply for Policy?', Cato Policy Analysis 590 (11 April 2007).

6 B. Stevenson and J. Wolfers, 'Economic Growth and Subjective Well-being: Reassessing the Easterlin Paradox', National Bureau of Economic Research working paper (2008).

7 Sara J. Solnick and David Hemenway, 'Is More Always Better? A Survey on Positional Concerns', *Journal of Economic Behavior & Organization* 37:3 (30 November 1998), pp. 373–83.

8 Bill Frelick, 'Bhutan's Ethnic Cleansing', *Human Rights Watch News*, 2 February 2008: http://www.hrw.org/news/2008/01/31/ bhutans-ethnic-cleansing

9 See in particular Daniel Kahneman and Alan B. Krueger, 'Developments in the Measurement of Subjective Well-being', *Journal of Economic Perspectives* 20:1 (2006), pp. 3–24.

10 Daniel Kahneman and Angus Deaton, 'High Income Improves Evaluation of Life but not Emotional Well-being', *PNAS*, 7 September 2010.

13 Can growth continue for ever?

1 Tom Murphy, 'Exponential Economist Meets Finite Physicist', *Do The Math* blog: physics.ucsd.edu/do-the-math/2012/04/ economist-meets-physicist/

2 Mark Aguiar and Eric Hurst, 'Measuring Trends in Leisure: The Allocation of Time over Five Decades', Federal Reserve Bank of Boston Working Paper 06-02 (2006): http://www.bos. frb.org/economic/wp/wp2006/wp0602.pdf

14 Inequality

1 Ruth Alexander, 'Dollar Benchmark: The Rise of the Dollar a Day Statistic', *BBC Online Magazine*, 9 March 2012: http://www.bbc.co.uk/news/magazine-17312819

2 John Cassidy, 'Relatively Deprived', *New Yorker*, 3 April 2006.

3 Thomas Gabe, 'Poverty in the United States: 2011', Congressional Research Service Report for Congress, 27 September 2012: http://www.fas.org/sgp/crs/misc/RL33069.pdf

4 University of York Social Policy Research Unit, 'The Measurement of Absolute Poverty (E2/SEP/14/2000)', p. 31, Table 2.17: http://www.york.ac.uk/inst/spru/research/pdf/AbsolutePoverty.pdf

5 Jonathan Portes, 'Neighbours from Hell: Who is the Prime Minister Talking About?', *Not the Treasury View*, 17 February 2012: http://notthetreasuryview.blogspot.co.uk/2012/02/families-from-hell-who-is-prime.html

6 'Perry Preschool Project', Social Programs that Work website: http://evidencebasedprograms.org/1366-2/65-2

7 Branko Milanovic, 'Global Inequality by the Numbers: In history and now', World Bank Policy Research Working Paper 6259 (November 2012): http://www-wds.worldbank.org/external/default/WDSContentServer/IW3P/IB/2012/11/06/000158349_20121106085546/Rendered/PDF/wps6259.pdf

8 CIA, *World Factbook*, consulted March 2013: https://www.cia.gov/library/publications/the-world-factbook/fields/2172.html

9 *The Economist*, 15 December 2012: http://www.economist.com/news/finance-and-economics/21568423-new-survey-illuminates-extent-chinese-income-inequality-each-not

10 Bloomberg News, 'China's Richer-Than-Romney Lawmakers Reveal Reform Challenge', 7 March 2013: http://www.bloomberg.com/news/2013-03-06/china-s-richer-than-romney-lawmakers-show-xi-s-reform-challenge.html

11 Emmanuel Saez, 'Striking It Richer: The Evolution of Top Incomes in the United States' (23 January 2013), Table 1: http://elsa.berkeley.edu/~saez/saez-UStopincomes-2011.pdf

12 Anthony Atkinson, Thomas Piketty and Emmanual Saez, 'Top Incomes in the Long Run of History', *Journal of Economic*

Literature 49:1 (2011), pp. 3–71: http://elsa.berkeley.edu/~saez/atkinson-piketty-saezJEL10.pdf

13 Timothy Noah, 'The Great Divergence', *Slate*, 3 September 2010: http://img.slate.com/media/3/100914_NoahT_Great Divergence.pdf

15 The future of macroeconomics

1 'New Model Army', *The Economist*, 19 January 2013: http://www.economist.com/news/finance-and-economics/21569752-efforts-are-under-way-improve-macroeconomic-models-new-model-army

2 There are some high-profile exceptions, such as Markus Brunnermeier of Princeton, or William White (now retired) and Claudio Borio of the Bank for International Settlements. There are also microeconomists who have been drawn into macroeconomics because of their interest in the financial system, such as Hyun Shin of Princeton and John Geanakoplos of Yale.

3 See J. Barkley Rosser Jr, 'On the Complexities of Complex Economic Dynamics', *Journal of Economic Perspectives* 13:4 (Fall 1999), pp. 169–92.

4 See Henry Petroski, *Success through Failure: The Paradox of Design* (Princeton, NJ: Princeton University Press, 2008); Mattys Levi and Mario Salvadori, *Why Buildings Fall Down* (New York: W.W. Norton, 1994).

5 On the subject of the Millennium Bridge, see Steven Strogatz, Daniel Abrams, Allan McRobie, Bruno Eckhardt and Edward Ott, 'Theoretical Mechanics: Crowd Synchrony on the Millennium Bridge', *Nature* 438 (3 November 2005), pp. 43–4; Steve Strogatz's TED talk, 'Strogatz on Sync' (2004): http://www.ted.com/talks/steven_strogatz_on_sync.html

Index

Also by Tim Harford

THE UNDERCOVER
ECONOMIST

'Reading this book is like spending an ordinary day
wearing X-ray goggles'
David Bodanis

'Required reading ... it brings the power of economics to life'
Steven D. Levitt, co-author of *Freakonomics*

Ever wondered why the gap between rich and poor nations is
so great, or why it's so difficult getting a foot on the property
ladder, or how to outwit Starbucks? This book offers the hidden
story behind these and other questions, as economist Tim
Harford reveals how supermarkets, airlines, and coffee chains –
to name just a few – are vacuuming money from our wallets.

Written with a light, humorous touch but backed up by
the latest economic research, this eye-opening book
exposes the forces that shape our day-to-day lives,
often without our knowing it.

DEAR UNDERCOVER ECONOMIST

Are there tangible benefits in flossing? Is it wrong to fake orgasms? What does the perfect online dating ad look like? Should we bother doing the ironing? Is it really impossible to buy the perfect Christmas gift? (Other than this book, of course.)

Economists might not be the first people you would think of to give you advice on such diverse areas as parenting, the intricacies of etiquette or the dark arts of seduction. But for years bestselling author Tim Harford has been doing just that: answering the most challenging questions in his brilliant column, where he uses the tools of economics to give practical advice about everyday dilemmas, conundrums and concerns. From family rows and the stock market to buying socks or speed dating, you'll find within these pages a witty – and of course rational – explanation for almost everything you ever wanted to know about life.

THE LOGIC OF LIFE: UNCOVERING THE NEW ECONOMICS OF EVERYTHING

'Truly eye-opening ... There is almost no situation that Harford cannot dissect with his sharp economist's tools ... economics has never been this cool'
New Statesman

If humans are so clever, why do we smoke and gamble, or take drugs, or fall in love? Is this really rational behaviour? And how come your idiot boss is so overpaid? In fact, the behaviour of even the unlikeliest of individuals – prostitutes, drug addicts, racists and revolutionaries – complies with economic logic, taking into account future costs and benefits, even if we don't quite realise it. We are rational beings after all.

ADAPT:
WHY SUCCESS ALWAYS STARTS WITH FAILURE

'An excellent book full of insight and surprise ...
I wish I had written this book'
Evan Davis

Everything we know about solving the world's
problems is wrong.

Out: Plans, experts and above all, leaders.

In: Adapting – improvise rather than plan; fail,
learn, and try again

In *Adapt*, Tim Harford shows how the world's most complex
and important problems – including terrorism, climate change,
poverty, innovation, and the financial crisis – can only be solved
from the bottom up by rapid experimenting and adapting.

From a spaceport in the Mojave Desert to the street battles of
Iraq, from a blazing offshore drilling rig to everyday decisions in
our business and personal lives, this is a handbook for surviving –
and prospering – in our complex and ever-shifting world.

To buy any of our books and to find out
more about Abacus and Little, Brown, our authors
and titles, as well as events and book clubs,
visit our website

www.littlebrown.co.uk

and follow us on Twitter

@AbacusBooks
@LittleBrownUK

To order any Abacus titles p & p free in the UK,
please contact our mail order supplier on:

+ 44 (0)1832 737525

Customers not based in the UK should contact
the same number for appropriate postage
and packing costs.